Strong Managers, Strong Owners

The family firm preparing generational change, the partnership that welcomes new partners, and the shareholders of a firm that chooses to go public are making decisions that will have an impact on strategy and management. Conversely, a change in strategy such as a move to diversify or a decision to take on more risk in a business can make the firm more attractive to some shareholders and less attractive to others and is therefore not ownership neutral. Opening the black box of agency theory, Korine and Gomez show how management and ownership interact to shape the strategy of the firm. In their view, the critical question to ask is not what is the best strategy, but rather, who is the strategy for? With numerous detailed examples, *Strong Managers, Strong Owners* is an invaluable resource for company owners, board members, and executives, as well as their advisors in strategy and governance.

HARRY KORINE is an Adjunct Professor of Strategy at INSEAD. As an educator, consultant, and public speaker, he engages with executives, board members, and owners to address questions of strategy development and long-term value generation, especially in a multinational context. Together with Pierre-Yves Gomez, he is the author of *Entrepreneurs and Democracy: A Political Theory of Corporate Governance* (Cambridge University Press, 2008).

PIERRE-YVES GOMEZ is Professor of Strategic Management at EM Lyon Business School (France) and Director of the French Corporate Governance Institute. His research focuses on the political foundations of corporate governance, as well as collective utility functions and their application to strategy and governance. He has published several award-winning books in French and English.

Strong Managers, Strong Owners

Corporate Governance and Strategy

HARRY KORINE
INSEAD

PIERRE-YVES GOMEZ
EM Lyon

CAMBRIDGE
UNIVERSITY PRESS

CAMBRIDGE
UNIVERSITY PRESS

University Printing House, Cambridge CB2 8BS, United Kingdom

Published in the United States of America by Cambridge University Press, New York

Cambridge University Press is part of the University of Cambridge.

It furthers the University's mission by disseminating knowledge in the pursuit of education, learning and research at the highest international levels of excellence.

www.cambridge.org
Information on this title: www.cambridge.org/9781107044203

© Harry Korine and Pierre-Yves Gomez 2014

First published 2014

Printed in the United Kingdom by CPI Group Ltd, Croydon CR0 4YY

A catalogue record for this publication is available from the British Library

Library of Congress Cataloguing in Publication data
Korine, Harry, 1962–
Strong managers, strong owners : corporate governance and strategy /
Harry Korine & Pierre-Yves Gomez.
pages   cm
Includes bibliographical references and index.
ISBN 978-1-107-04420-3 (hardback)
1. Organizational change.   2. Corporate governance.   3. Executive
succession.   4. Strategic planning.   5. Management.
I. Gomez, Pierre-Yves.   II. Title.
HD58.8.K644 2013
658.4′012–dc23   2013022100

ISBN 978-1-107-04420-3 Hardback

Contents

Figures

Tables

Foreword

The interrelationships among shareholders, directors, and senior executives have come under the microscope only fairly recently. Having been personally involved in various capacities through the last two decades both on the public and private sides, I have seen first hand how the roles have evolved over time. Shareholders' awareness of their interests and rights, and their expectations of the people they have put in place to act in, if not protect their interests, have heightened over time, no doubt thanks to the numerous episodes of wide-scale frauds by executives or failure to discharge fiduciary duty by directors. To a similar extent, directors are now acutely aware of the onerous liabilities they assume when consenting to sit on boards. Heavier emphasis is being placed on appointing a rising proportion of nonexecutive or even independent directors, thereby subjecting the board-management relationship to even more tension. In short, the distinction between roles is being sharpened, and the lines of responsibility are more clearly drawn.

More critically, I am convinced that strategy formulation is never accidental; it is in fact the direct consequence of the interplay of the different interests among shareholders, directors, and management. This implies that any change in the composition of ownership or management can potentially have an impact on strategy. By the same token, if the strategy were refined or radically revamped, particularly with outside help, the dynamics between the shareholders and management would undoubtedly be affected.

We are all familiar with the experiences of a redefinition of strategy around a change in ownership, resulting from a merger or acquisition. I have witnessed first hand and twice over, as a senior executive in financial services, how the new owners reshaped strategy – defining what was core business, which strong market position to build on – and essentially restructuring the management teams along with the new priorities. Likewise, when a new investor such as a private equity fund takes on a significant shareholder role, the revised strategy will be consistent with and reflect the basis for investment, for example to realize value-add through operational enhancements or organic growth. In such circumstances, new chemistry and new working relationships have to be fostered. When managed carefully and sensitively, a stronger entity with a clearly defined business focus, executed by competent executives, should emerge.

This should hypothetically be no different even if the owner were a sovereign wealth fund. In reality, however, for businesses with a political or strategic element, say in the provision of public goods or essential services, more often than not, any shift in strategy may entail or even arise from noncommercial considerations. The more ambiguous the objectives for strategy review are, the greater the tension between owners and management will be.

It gets more complicated when government is a direct shareholder. I have come to realize that a deep appreciation of the multiple roles that a government can play is essential to understanding the impact of any strategy change on management. What are the factors giving rise to the typical confusion over the capacity that a government is acting in?

There is often more than meets the eye; this describes the unique situation where the government is both an owner and regulator and, in some cases, a customer as well! The arena of public goods is replete with illustrations of the tightrope that many governments walk on. Say in the area of public transportation or education or healthcare. The harsh reality is that these multiple roles have conflicting interests from time to time. As a regulator, the government may elect to have a more liberal competition framework for pay TV but the operator that it owns may well wish that competitive pressures are limited. Or that public policy may be leaning towards higher co-payments for nonessential healthcare services but competitive pressure limits what people pay. Whither the strategy in such circumstances?

Any public policy shift will necessarily lead to a corresponding redefinition of strategy of the state-owned business that plays in that space. This in turn requires a slew of changes that management will have to conceive, embrace, and execute, sometimes to better outcomes and, other times, with disastrous results. Occasionally, it's the opposite – where government assumes a doctrinaire position as a shareholder but the underlying market transformation warrants a new strategy. Something has to give; if the government insists on no change in stance despite market indications to the contrary, then management will be saddled with the burden of treading carefully between pleasing the owner and staying relevant. Overall, I have observed that it will serve governments well to adopt a dynamic stance towards its participation in business.

Where government is a shareholder, many relevant questions are posed – should it remain involved in business? If not, when should the exit be? What form should its involvement take – active or purely financial? This is a topic of immense interest to many, including myself, and especially those who have to deal with either the state bureaucracy or state-owned enterprises.

It will be futile to push for a convergence of interests across owners, board members, and management because such an outcome does not always exist. Instead, I have learnt that it would be more pragmatic to understand the differences, some of which are inherent in the definition of roles, and to accept that the desired outcome has necessarily to be multidimensional. There would be competing and conflicting demands on resources or simply a difference in expectations. But ultimately, the long-term, sustainable well-being of the firm must reign supreme. In any course of action or revision to strategy, we must always bear in mind that making tradeoffs and minimizing tension and power play should be part and parcel of such an exercise.

Strong Managers, Strong Owners, by Korine and Gomez, reflects a deep understanding of how the potential differences among the various stakeholders' interests can influence the shaping of strategy. It offers simple but sound advice on how to take these multiple interests into consideration when formulating strategy.

Lim Hwee Hua
Former Minister in the Prime Minister's Office in Singapore
Executive Director, Tembusu Partners Private Equity Limited,
Singapore

Acknowledgments

This book has been three years in the making and draws on over ten years of joint research. Over such a long period of time, we have benefitted from the ideas and support of many.

We would first like to thank our respective academic homes, INSEAD and EM Lyon. In addition, we want to express our appreciation to Professor Dominic Houlder of the London Business School for encouraging the Sloan graduate course upon which some of the materials in this book are based, to Professor Quy Huy of INSEAD for offering the stimulus of challenging discussions about strategy research, and the French Institute of Corporate Governance at EM Lyon for financial support. The important contribution of successive generations of London Business School Sloan Fellows is gratefully acknowledged, as is the input of numerous named and unnamed senior corporate decision-makers who shared their experiences with us. A special thank you goes finally to Bernhard Kerres and Valerie Mars, senior executive sounding boards for the ideas presented in this book.

We appreciate the steadfast support of our editor, Paula Parish, of Cambridge University Press. In many ways, this new book represents a further development and a systematic application of the theoretical framework we first presented in *Entrepreneurs and Democracy* in 2008. This is why it is especially nice to have been able to work again with the same publisher and the same editor.

Introduction

Is there one best strategy in any given situation, or does it depend on whom the strategy is for? This question should be at the heart of every discussion about strategy. Consider the well-known story of Deutsche Börse's failed effort to take over the London Stock Exchange (LSE) in 2005.[1] Whereas German institutional shareholders generally supported the cross-border consolidation strategy proposed by CEO Dr. Werner Seifert and approved by the supervisory board, a group of non-German hedge funds led by TCI (The Children's Investment Fund Management) and Atticus Capital decided to actively oppose the strategic direction of the firm and campaign that the money be used instead for a share repurchase program. Over a period of three months, TCI and other opponents of the consolidation strategy were able to gain enough influence over the shareholding body to persuade management to withdraw the offer for the LSE, agree to a share repurchase, and to force the replacement of Dr. Seifert and the resignation of Dr. Rolf-E. Breuer, chairman of the supervisory board. Triggered by an attempt to raise the stakes and make Deutsche Börse a leading global player, the LSE episode in fact brought about a change in the balance of power among shareholders, resulting in a strategic about-face and a change in the leadership of the firm. Ironically, of all firms not to take the diverse interests of shareholders into account in the making of strategy, with Deutsche Börse it was a stock exchange that suffered one of recent history's most remarkable reversals at the hands of a group of shareholders determined to defend *their* view of the right strategy.

In general, researchers and practitioners work with the assumption that the choice of the right strategy does not depend on the interests of the actors involved: there is one economically best strategy for the firm.[2] If, however, shareholders differ among themselves and differ with managers in terms of their preferences as described in the case of Deutsche Börse, then what is best for one subgroup may not be good, or even acceptable, for others. Depending on which coalition emerges as dominant, strategic choices may in fact impair the long-term prospects of the firm. If strategy is not neutral – that is, not purely economic, but determined by a political process with its own rationality – then we cannot avoid asking the question, "strategy for whom?"

Background

The founder of a family firm who transfers ownership to his/her children, the partnership that welcomes new partners, and the shareholders of a firm that chooses to go public are making decisions that are not merely legal or financial, but also strategic. Conversely, a change in strategy such as a move to diversify or a decision to take on more risk in a business can make the firm more attractive to some shareholders and less attractive to others and is therefore not ownership neutral. And yet, in academic research, ownership and strategy are treated separately: finance and law deal with the roles and rights of shareholders; economics and behavioral perspectives explain a firm's strategic choices of resource allocation and competitive position. The separation between ownership and strategy is mirrored in the professional services that address these topics: investment banks and law firms for ownership, general management consultants for strategy. Business school education perpetuates the divide, presenting ownership as a stand-alone topic or as an aspect of corporate finance and only very rarely making more than a passing reference to ownership in strategy courses, *as if* ownership and strategy were entirely unrelated.

In 1932, Berle (a scholar in corporate law) and Means (an economist) wrote a very influential book about the separation of ownership and control (over strategy) in American publicly listed firms.[3] They observed that shareholdings had become more dispersed and shareholders less influential over time and that control over strategic decisions in the firm had effectively been transferred to nonshareholder managers. The work of Berle and Means marked the beginning of the separation of ownership and strategy in academic research and provided the empirical basis for the development of agency theory.[4] In agency theory, the firm is described as consisting of principals (read shareholders) who provide capital and do not get involved in strategy and their agents (read management) who make decisions for the firm. Because the interests of shareholders (maximizing return to shareholders) and managers (maximizing return to management) may lead to opposite conclusions in practice, agency theory predicts conflict between shareholders and managers and emphasizes the need to align the interests of the two groups by means of incentives.

Separating questions of ownership and strategy was undoubtedly appropriate in the heyday of the management profession. Nonshareholder management dominated strategic decision-making in many companies and in many countries for most of the twentieth century, especially in the case of publicly listed firms.[5] But what about today – is the separation between ownership and strategy still justified? Globalization and technological development have rendered competitive advantage fleeting and undermined the dominance of management; the concomitant growth of capital markets has made firms more dependent on outside capital. As a result, the shareholders of publicly listed firms have become more influential, both indirectly, through the force of expectations and the threat of sale, and directly, through activist intervention, as described in the case of Deutsche Börse above.[6] In privately held firms, shareholders never did go away: even in those private firms where nonshareholder managers were put in charge, the influence of the family or the partners always had to be reckoned with, and this is still true today.

Of course, nonshareholder management continues to play a very important role in strategic decision-making, both in publicly listed and in privately held firms. Except in those firms where a shareholder is also the chief executive, nonshareholder managers are formally responsible for formulating and implementing strategy. What has changed over the last thirty years in both the publicly listed and the private firm is not the formal role of the nonshareholder manager, but the way the role is played out: not in opposition to shareholders and their interests as propounded by agency theory, but in full recognition of the interests of ownership.

Theory

In this book, we depart from the key agency theoretic assumption of uniform interests among shareholders.[7] Based on an emerging perspective in the corporate governance and finance literatures and our own research, we posit that shareholders differ among themselves in terms of their values – that is to say the relative measures that they use to evaluate their own performance. Thus, whereas some shareholders orient themselves towards an external value such as equity market and peer group performances indices, other shareholders look to an internal value such as the continuity of the firm and what it stands for. Not only do shareholders have different values, they also have different methods, with some seeking to vocally influence decision-making, while others remain silent and primarily influence strategy by the threat of sale. This makes it doubly important to insist upon a detailed assessment of the shareholding structure in interpreting the relationship between ownership and strategy.

Shareholders may be diverse, but what about managers – can one assume that the managers of the same executive group have the same values and operate according to the same methods?[8] As we will discuss in Chapter 2, a similar categorization as that applied to shareholders can be applied to managers, distinguishing among those who follow a value defined outside the firm (i.e., financial market expectations or professional standards) and those who adhere to a value defined inside the firm and among those whose method tends towards rupture and those whose method tends towards continuity. This book will argue that explaining how these differences among shareholders and among managers as well as between shareholders and managers play out is the key to developing an understanding of how ownership and management affect strategy.

It is critical to note that the relationships between ownership, management, and strategy are not readily apparent in a steady state; there are no simple correlations between types of ownership or types of management and types of strategy. The interpretation becomes easier if we focus on change events: in practice, changing *who directs* the firm has a definite impact on the *direction* the firm will take, and changing the *direction* of the firm has implications for the question of *who* will *direct* the firm. In the general case, diverse shareholders with different values and different methods confront diverse executives with their own values and methods.[9]

As depicted in Figure 0.1 below, conflict over strategy can occur both *between* shareholders as a group and executives as a group (as predicted by agency theory) as well as *among* shareholders and *among* executives. Strategy choices result from the emergence of dominant coalitions between diverse shareholders and diverse executives. Thus, a change in the identity of ownership just as much as a change in the identity of the chief executive and his/her team can lead to a reconsideration of strategy. A change of strategy, in turn, may well engender changes in the identity of ownership and of management, as disgruntled shareholders or executives unsuited to the new strategy

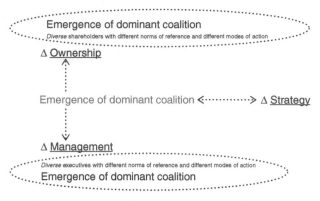

Figure 0.1 Ownership, management, and strategy.

leave the firm. The interaction of firm ownership, management, and strategy allows a dominant coalition of shareholders and managers to emerge and determines the future of the firm.

In every firm, ownership, management, and strategy are embedded in a system of corporate governance – procedures and controls that serve to ensure the accountability of the decision-makers.[10] We speak of the corporate governance of leading change to emphasize the point that significant changes in ownership, management, and (or) strategy can stretch the firm's existing system of corporate governance and be the cause of major governance failures: new shareholders can substitute short-term opportunism for long-term profit maximization; new management can divert resources for pet projects or personal gain; and new strategy can be the source of significant new risk. In practice, leading change successfully depends on adapting the firm's system of corporate governance to ensure control and maintain accountability. The board of directors, in our framing, is one of, if not the most important locations for addressing the conflicts among and between shareholders and managers. In most jurisdictions, the board of directors is called upon to act in the best long-term interest of the firm.[11] In practice, this is impossible to define precisely, and, given diverse shareholders and diverse managers with different perspectives on what constitutes the best long-term interest of the firm, the board of directors has to deal with the reality that strategy is created by the interaction of these different perspectives.

In opening the black box of agency theory to consider how shareholders and managers differ among themselves, and in exploring how decisions are made when these actors come to different conclusions about the direction of the firm, we present a political picture of strategy.[12] In our view, strategic choices are the outcome of a political process and, in turn, create a new political reality, strengthening some, weakening others, and, if the firm's ownership and management structures are open, in due course attracting new shareholders and new managers. Such a political picture of strategy goes against the received wisdom of strategy as rational choice: if strategy is the outcome of a political process, then it is the preferred solution only for a circumscribed group. In our analysis of strategic decisions, the critical question to ask is not what is the best strategy, but rather, who is the strategy for.

Outline

The arguments presented in this book build upon our collective research efforts in ownership, management, and strategy. We have observed a relationship between ownership change and strategy change in a broad range of cases: privately held firms and publicly listed firms; small firms and large firms; European, American, and Asian firms. Chapters 1 and 2 explore the effects of changes in the identity of ownership and in the identity of management. We find that changes in the identity of ownership can have significant effects on management and strategy. Changes in the identity of management, in turn, have far-reaching effects not only on strategy, but also on ownership and governance. Chapters 3 and 4 examine the special cases of changes in form: of the legal structure and of the organization. We find that any change in form has implications for strategy, whether it is brought about by sharing decision-making power with new actors, as in the case of an initial public offering (IPO), or by redistributing power among existing actors, as in the case of an internal reorganization.

Strategy change events – in corporate strategy and in business strategies – are covered in Chapter 5. Changes in strategy affect ownership and management in light of the institutional challenges and informational requirements posed by the strategy: the more important the change in strategy, the greater the potential impact. These effects are not automatic, however, and changes in strategy can be interpreted as struggles for power over the direction of the firm. Now, changes in strategy are usually also associated with changes in the fortunes of a firm; in fact, success in the marketplace is the ultimate measure of the suitability of a strategy.[13] In the context of examining changes in strategy, it is therefore also of interest to examine under what performance conditions change may be *blocked*: Chapter 6 looks at cases where no changes occur in ownership, management, and strategy – *despite failure* in the marketplace; Chapter 7 studies examples in which market *success reinforces* the existing constellation of ownership, management, and strategy. When ownership, management, and strategy are closely interlinked, for example when they are all tied to the same person or if stakeholder groups are tightly connected, adaptation can be prevented.

Chapter 8 reviews the institutions of corporate governance, with particular emphasis on the challenges of leading change and the role of the board of directors. Is there one best strategy in any given situation, or does it depend on whom the strategy is for? We return to this question in the Conclusion and outline the practical and theoretical implications of considering strategy not as neutral, but as driven by different interests.

Purpose

This book is intended for company owners, board members, and executives considering changes in firm ownership, management, or strategy, as well as the professionals in governance (lawyers, auditors, and investment bankers) and general management (consultants) who advise them. Compared to the specialist approaches of lawyers and consultants, the added value of our cross-disciplinary perspective lies in pointing out the broader consequences of apparently narrow legal or strategic actions. Our hope is that reading this book will lead more firms and their advisors to consider the interactions between ownership, management, and strategy when they devise plans for change. Inasmuch as whole industries may change ownership form and subsequently choose a different, more risky strategic emphasis, such as was the case for the great US investment banks whose governance histories are discussed in Chapter 3, policy makers may also find food for thought. Most importantly, we want to persuade the worlds of academia and business to do away with the time-honored illusion that firm ownership, management, and strategy can be considered in isolation from one another.

Background reading – Introduction

Berle, A. A. and Means, G. C. *The Modern Corporation and Private Property*, New York: Transaction Publishers, 1932.

Gomez, P. -Y. and Korine, H. *Entrepreneurs and Democracy: A Political Theory of Corporate Governance*, Cambridge University Press, 2008.

Hofer, P. and Schendel, D. *Strategy Formulation: Analytical Concepts*, St. Paul: West Publishing Company, 1978.

Monks, R. A. G. and Minow. N. *Corporate Governance* (second edn.), Oxford: Blackwell, 2001.

Porter, M. *Competitive Strategy*, New York: Free Press, 1980.

Roe, M. J. *Strong Managers, Weak Owners: The Political Roots of American Corporate Finance*, Princeton University Press, 1994.

Rumelt, R. P. *Good Strategy Bad Strategy*, New York: Crown Business, 2011.

Solomon, J. and Solomon, A. *Corporate Governance and Accountability*, Chichester: Wiley, 2004.

PART I

Changes in the identity of ownership and management

In the standard principal agent formulation of the relationship between ownership and management, there is no need to analyze the identity of ownership and management: as set out in the introductory discussion of agency theory, shareholders all are interested in maximizing the value of the firm, and managers all are interested in maximizing their personal wealth. The question of identity only becomes relevant if we allow for differences among shareholders and differences among managers. In the following two chapters, we will propose one framework for differentiating among shareholders and another, similar framework for differentiating among managers. These two frameworks permit us to draw a more nuanced picture of shareholders and managers and to show how changes in the identities of shareholders and managers affect strategy and governance.

ONE

Change in ownership

The impact of a change in the identity of ownership is of concern to all firms. Every family business has to think about what might happen when the next generation assumes ownership of the firm; every partnership frets over the consequences of bringing in new partners; cooperatives and associations wonder whether the entry of new members will upset the prevailing balance of interests; and, of course, listed companies keep a careful eye on their shareholder rosters to detect changes that might imply a challenge for control.

I. The purpose of shareholders

In order to understand why changes in the identity of ownership are so important to firms no matter what the form of ownership, we need to start with an explanation of the purpose of shareholders in capitalism. Obviously, shareholders provide capital, but so do banks and trade creditors, and even employees, in the form of human capital. The finance literature emphasizes that the capital provided by shareholders is noncontractual – that shareholders are residual claimants who are only paid if there remains a profit after all other creditors have been satisfied. This defines the type of capital provided by shareholders, but it does not explain their purpose. Why is there a need for residual claimants? The contours of an answer can be found in the distant history of the corporation. As

Keynes pointed out in his *General Theory of Employment, Interest, and Money* (1936: Book 4, Chapter 12), shareholders in the original stock corporations of the seventeenth and eighteenth centuries provided capital that might be *irrevocably lost*. The collected capital of multiple shareholders is what allowed highly risky ventures such as shipping or trading to be pursued on a large scale. Through their practically irrevocable engagement, shareholders established a general level of *confidence* in these ventures that would otherwise not have been launched.

Of course, today's shareholders commitment of capital is rarely irrevocable. However, the purpose of establishing and maintaining confidence in the firm remains. Consider the firm whose shareholders all want to sell at the same time: this signals an extreme loss of confidence in the firm. Conversely, shareholders who stay represent a nucleus of stability around which the firm can develop long-term plans. If shareholders provide *stability* essential to the firm, then it is clear that any change in the shareholding body has implications for the strategy. Shareholders buy into a particular perspective on the future. Once some of them decide to disengage or that perspective changes, the basis for confidence in the firm changes, and the strategy is necessarily affected. The case of Europe's largest travel group, TUI AG, a German firm that has gone through multiple changes in the identity of ownership and multiple changes in corporate strategy over the last sixty years concisely illustrates the importance of considering how changes in ownership and changes in strategy are related.

TUI – *changing ownership, changing strategy*

The TUI travel group traces its origins back to the "Preußische Bergwerks- und Hütten-Aktiengesellschaft" (later shortened to Preussag), a coal and steel company founded in 1923. In 1959, Preussag became the very first state-owned German firm to be privatized, when 77 percent of the shares were placed with the public (the federal government retaining the remaining shares through its VEBA holding until 1970 when VEBA itself was privatized). Strict allocation and income restrictions were placed on these privatizations in order to ensure that the shares would reach a majority of the people (thus the sobriquet "Volksaktie," or people's share) and that ownership would not be concentrated. Today, forty years after the final privatization, ownership of the firm is concentrated in the hands of Norwegian shipping magnate John Frederiksen (15 percent) and several smaller activist stakes, on the one hand, and a group of different travel interests (Russian entrepreneur Alexej Mordashow through his S-Travel firm, 25 percent, the state of Morocco, 15 percent, and Spanish RIU Hotels, 5 percent), on the other. These different shareholders have been battling each other over strategy and governance questions since 2008.

Over the years since the initial privatizations, ownership changes at Preussag (now TUI) have been followed by strategy changes that have in turn brought about further ownership changes and renewed discussions about strategy. Following its release from state control, Preussag diversified into a variety of fields, chemicals, logistics, electricity, and consumer goods, while maintaining its bases in coal and steel. By the early 1970s, the Westdeutsche Landesbank (26 percent of outstanding shares) and the Swedish mining firm Boliden (50 percent of Preussag's lead and zinc mining operations) had acquired considerable ownership in the firm and, under the influence of the oil crisis and with a new management in place, helped push through a refocus on the core mining and steel businesses. From the mid 1970s through the early 1990s, Preussag pursued international expansion in mining, and once the steel business was back on track (from 1981) diversified once more, this time into construction engineering and ship building, as well as deepening its holdings in oil and natural gas.

In 1989, Preussag converted itself into a holding company comprised of four legally independent business units centered on its four core businesses: coal, crude oil, natural gas, and plant construction and then merged with the fifty-year-old, state-held steel and real estate conglomerate Salzgitter AG, creating a DM27 billion behemoth employing 70,000 workers.[1] Proceeds from the sale of parts of Salzgitter's real estate portfolio permitted the further expansion of Preussag into fields as diverse as limestone, oil drilling, automobile recycling, mining transport, plaster board, industrial freight forwarding, lead oxide, transport services, engineering, and even telecommunications and further internationalization to 48 percent of sales by 1995. At the same time, the firm initiated a series of divestments in an effort to concentrate on its "core competences," before CEO Michael Frenzel in 1996 launched a radical change in corporate strategy and entered the tourism industry with the acquisition of Hapag Lloyd. This was followed by a series of smaller purchases in tourism – First Travel, Thomson Travel, and Nouvelles Frontières – and the sale, in 1998, of the original steel business (including Salzgitter AG). By 2002, Preussag Energy had also been sold, and the firm that had severed almost every link with its history of coal and steel would be appropriately renamed TUI (standing for Touristik Union Internazionale).[2]

The new focus on tourism also brought in new industrial shareholders, the first of which was RIU Hotels which took over the remaining 5 percent of Westdeutsche Landesbank's historic shareholding in 2004. With the tacit support of these new shareholders, TUI in 2005 spent €2.1 billion to acquire CP ships and make shipping its second major leg. Coming after several years of disappointing profit figures, the move into shipping was enough to draw the attention of the Hermes Focus Funds and DWS which purchased small stakes (<1 percent) and first publicly demanded the breakup of TUI in 2006. Subsequently, two other well-known activists from the world of finance, Guy Wyser-Pratte and Florian Homm, also joined the fray. In part to fend off the activists' attack on the management (still Michael Frenzel), the supervisory board, and the strategy of TUI, the Egyptian Mohamed el Chiaty and the Moroccan state were invited to buy major blocks of shares in 2007 (3 percent and 5 percent, respectively). These were industrial shareholders like RIU Hotels, with a desire to secure the flow of German tourists to their resorts. The battle among shareholders over strategy calmed down somewhat, but only until Norwegian shipping magnate John Frederiksen acquired a 15 percent stake in 2008 and joined the activists in calling for a breakup of the firm (by a sale of its shipping arm) and a change in management. To counter this development, management and the board turned to another shareholder from the travel industry, the Russian firm S-Travel (controlled by Alexej Mordachow), who joined the shareholding body in 2008 and has since become the biggest single shareholder at 25 percent. In 2010, finally, TUI sold off its shipping business, to concentrate once more on travel.

A purely strategic analysis of the post-War evolution of Preussag and subsequently TUI would identify alternating phases of diversification and refocusing. This is a firm that has always been involved in highly cyclical industries and seems to have made a habit (especially pronounced in the last two decades) of buying into new sectors at the top of the cycle and selling out of other sectors at the bottom. What is the logic of these moves that defy conventional wisdom of what makes good strategic sense and have transformed the value proposition of the firm several times?[3] At one level, the evolution of Preussag (and later TUI) has simply mirrored the trends of its times: diversification in the booming 1960s, refocusing in the austerity of the 1970s, diversification again in the opening markets of the 1980s and 1990s (coupled with internationalization), and a radical departure to enter seemingly more future-oriented businesses after 1996. Other conglomerates have also followed these trends, although few, if any, with the zeal displayed by Preussag (TUI). At another level, the evolution of the firm also reflects the ambitions of its managers, especially Erwin Moeller (CEO from 1989) and Michael Frenzel (CEO from 1993). Susceptibility to trends and ambitious managers certainly played a role in the history of the firm, but do not explain why the shareholding structure has changed so often and so dramatically, nor do they shed light on the question of why so many different types of shareholders have at one time or another become involved with the firm.

The story of Preussag (TUI) can also be told from the point of view of the shareholders that have at different times influenced the strategy of the firm. From federal government and the house bank, Westdeutsche Landesbank (WLB), to different types of industrial shareholders (from tourism, later also from shipping) and activists from the world of finance, many different types of shareholders have played important roles in shaping the course of the firm. Partial privatization (in 1959) opened the door to diversification, and the poor results of diversification led to a period of dominance by the house bank which persisted into the 1990s. The moves into tourism and shipping, although initially supported by the house bank, eventually altered the shareholding structure, and today TUI is held in tenuous equilibrium by two very different types of shareholders with very different plans for the firm (support of tourism vs. breakup and sale). The history of the firm shows that each major change of ownership has been accompanied by a new strategy, and each major change of strategy has eventually led to a new shareholding structure. The last sixty years of Preussag (TUI) read like a continuous back and forth between changes in ownership and changes in strategy (summarized in Table 1.1 below).

With new shareholders came new strategies and with new strategies came new shareholders. Clearly, the federal government is not looking for the same things from its shareholding in a firm like Preussag as the house bank: it has a different perspective on ownership. Industrial shareholders in TUI like the state of Morocco and

TABLE 1.1 *From Preussag to TUI: sixty years of ownership change and strategy change*

Time	Ownership change	Strategy change
1959	Initial privatization	
1960s		Diversification (poor results)
By early 1970s	WLB and Boliden dominate	
From 1970s		Refocusing on steel, mining
From 1980s	Shares broadly dispersed	
From late 1980s		Salzgitter and diversification
From early 1990s	Government holding reduced	
From mid 1990s		Hapag Lloyd acquisition
From early 2000s	New tourism shareholders	
From mid 2000s		Further growth of shipping
From 2006	Activists & shipping interests	
2010		Exit shipping

activists like Guy Wyser-Pratte differ fundamentally in motivation and approach. Perhaps the reason why so many different types of shareholders have become involved with one and the same firm over time is that Preussag (TUI) has tried so many different strategies and been involved in so many diverse industries. The case shows that shareholders are not all alike and that different shareholders create different contexts for strategy. In order to understand how different types of shareholders influence a firm's strategy, it is necessary to take a step back and discuss what motivates different shareholders and how they exert influence.

Different types of shareholders

In this book, we depart from the key agency theoretic assumption of uniform interests among shareholders. For analytical convenience, shareholders are traditionally assumed to all want the same thing, namely the maximization of shareholder returns.[4] In the general case, the shareholding body of a listed firm can include many different kinds of actors: on the one hand, private individuals (retail), savings institutions such as pension funds and insurers, and financial intermediaries such as mutual funds and asset managers, who only have a shareholding relationship with the firm; and, on the other hand, employees, partner firms such as suppliers or customers, and institutions such as founder families and foundations who have both a shareholding and a business relationship with the firm. At a minimum, the latter type of shareholder has a more multifaceted relationship with the firm than the former and therefore has multiple interests to satisfy.[5] Moreover, there are differences even within these two subgroups: thus, institutional investors like pension funds differ among themselves in terms of which financial variables are important to them,[6] and the interests of those shareholders with a business relationship to the firm differ according to the nature of the business relationship. Therefore, if we wish to draw a nuanced picture of how shareholders behave with regards to strategy, we cannot maintain the assumption of uniform interests among shareholders.

Shareholders who only have a shareholding relationship with the firm will be concerned about questions such as liquidity and risk, in addition to return. Shareholders who also have a business relationship with the firm will include such questions as the satisfaction of business objectives (for shareholders who are also customers or suppliers), the stability of employment prospects (for employees), the maintenance of corporate values (for founder families and foundations), and the continuity of the firm in their objective functions, alongside the financial considerations. Instead of uniform interests, we have in fact a veritable plethora of different and apparently distinct interests to consider in analyzing how shareholders will respond to changes in strategy.

Point to watch: shareholders differ

One of the tenets of finance is that all shareholders want the same thing of the firm they are invested in, namely that it maximizes returns. There may be differences of opinion on how to achieve maximum returns, but in the end, it all boils down to the same thing for shareholders. This perspective ignores the very real differences that exist among shareholders for the sake of expediency – if there were more than one single objective for all shareholders, then the mathematical treatment of shareholder utility would be much more difficult. If, indeed, there are multiple and conflicting objectives among shareholders and these objectives are subject to negotiation, then it is impossible to conclude what the outcome will be in the general case. We acknowledge this difficulty and explicitly opt for descriptive accuracy over theoretical parsimony.

We propose that the different shareholder concerns can be meaningfully grouped according to the standards shareholders use to measure the performance of their holdings. Whereas some shareholders measure the performance of their holdings relative to external (market-based) benchmarks, others apply standards of their own definition. Thus, a pension fund will measure the shareholder return from a particular firm relative to the return it can obtain by investing in similar firms or in the market, while a founder family will measure shareholder return in terms of an absolute, self-defined standard such as "adequate return" for maintaining the family. Clearly, the concerns of relevance to all shareholders – return, liquidity, and risk – can be evaluated according to both relative and absolute standards; the concerns which are only of relevance to shareholders who also have a business relationship with the firm – satisfaction of business objectives, stability of employment prospects, maintenance of corporate culture and continuity of the firm – do not lend themselves well to comparison and are therefore typically evaluated according to an absolute standard.

More generally, we will say that some shareholders are oriented towards external *values*, while others abide by internal values. External values are market measures of interest in the firm – defined relative to the broader market for similar investments or to a particular index. Internal values are interests that are defined in absolute terms, in relation to the specific firm. The key point of practical distinction between shareholders guided by external and internal values in evaluating the performance of their holdings is the intention to exit: shareholders with internal values do not have the intention to exit in the foreseeable future; shareholders with external values, on the other hand, may stay with a firm for one day or for several years, but the possibility of exit (and thereby outperforming the market in relative terms) is always central to their calculations of interest in the firm (Table 1.2 presents examples of external and internal values).

Of course, in integrating so many different concerns, our argument also simplifies. Shareholders guided primarily by external values may also pay some attention to internal values (think of public pension funds investing in domestic companies, who need to balance concerns about relative rates of return with concerns about local employment) and shareholders guided primarily by internal values will not be completely insensitive to relative rates of return (think of industrial shareholders with a business interest in the focal firm). Moreover, shareholders may, in some situations, substitute external for internal values and vice versa (see below). In the main,

TABLE 1.2 *Firm ownership: values*

Values	External	- *Equity market performance index*
		- *Peer performance index*
	Internal	- *Continuity of the firm*
		- *Strength of the relationship to the firm*

however, the values that characterize different shareholders are pronounced and enduring. This is because values are deeply engrained in shareholders of all types. Participants in the financial markets, for example, are wedded to external values by their professional ethos and the nature of competition in the industry – this is why throwing a bone to employment concerns is so difficult for them; conversely, the founder families of many firms have developed strong internal values around concerns such as people and relationships, making it very hard for them to even countenance external values such as relative rates of return. The more pronounced the value differences among shareholders the higher potential for conflict.

Shareholders differ not only in terms of their values, but also in terms of their *methods*, that is the ways in which they try to influence the firm. The definition of method as we will use it draws on the finance and corporate governance literatures, building on the notion of voice: shareholders who try to determine the direction of the firm by intervening in the strategic decision-making process are "vocal"; shareholders who are "silent" do not participate in decision-making.[7] Whereas vocal shareholders influence the firm directly, the influence of silent shareholders is indirect and manifests itself in decision-makers' efforts to satisfy their expectations (Table 1.3 provides examples of typical vocal and silent methods, in order of increasing impact on management and strategy).

If we consider both values and methods in classifying shareholders, we find that four distinct categories emerge: *traders* who are silent and subscribe to external values (the majority of investment funds

TABLE 1.3 *Firm ownership: methods*

Methods	
Vocal	Silent
- *Work with decision-makers*	- *Review holdings*
- *Place board members, execs*	- *Announce expectations*
- *Present plans; make decisions*	- *Indicate threat to sell shares*

belong to this category), *activists* who are vocal, but also subscribe to external values (as exemplified by the Hermes Focus Funds or the Icahn funds), *entrepreneurs* who are also vocal, but subscribe to internal values (this is the case of the typical family shareholder in the family dominated firm or the state in a state-controlled firm), and *sleepers* who are silent and subscribe to internal values (as exemplified by industrial shareholders or family shareholders without a voice in the firm).[8] The utility of this kind of categorization will become apparent as the argument proceeds, but it is worth noting that the shareholder categories defined here are applicable to the ownership of both publicly listed and privately held firms. Clearly, traders and activists are prevalent in publicly listed firms and entrepreneurs and sleepers predominate in privately held firms, but activists can become entrepreneurs and take a firm private, while entrepreneurs and sleepers in privately held firms can metamorphose into activists and traders who seek to maximize the financial worth of their personal portfolios. In general, the influence of any one shareholder or shareholder type depends on the balance of power among shareholders and varies according to relative size and ability to persuade other shareholders (see Section III below). The four categories of firm ownership are set out in Table 1.4 and will be referred to henceforth in discussing differences among shareholders.

II. The entry of new shareholders

For private firms such as family businesses and partnerships, changes in the identity of ownership count among the most significant

TABLE 1.4 *Firm ownership: values and methods*

		Methods	
		Vocal	Silent
Values	External	- Activist	- Trader
	Internal	- Entrepreneur	- Sleeper

change events in the firms' histories. In the family business, a change
in the identity of ownership goes together with the passing of the
torch from one generation to the next and raises a whole host of
questions: is the new generation ready? Will the members of the new
generation be able to agree among themselves? In what direction
will the young(er) ones take the firm?[9] Pictet, the two-hundred-
year-old Geneva-based private bank that is both a family business
(there has always been at least one Pictet among the partners) and
a partnership (the firm is owned by the partners in office), picks a
new partner (owner) only once every five years on average, and the
current partners spend a long time vetting the candidate and thinking about the impact he/she will have on the firm. In the words of
Jacques de Saussure, senior partner:

> when there are only eight or nine owners [partners], and we all have
> to live with the decisions we make as a team, there is nothing more
> important than knowing the person really well. In this day and age
> of IPOs and fast riches, we have to think about the signal that the
> choice sends to employees: above all, the new partner entrusted with
> a share in the ownership of the firm should stand for continuity.[10]

Depending on the inclinations and the influence of the new shareholders, strategy may stay the same or it may change, sometimes
radically. No observer of North American business can forget how a
change of generations in the Bronfman family turned the erstwhile
spirits giant Seagram into a producer of movies, or how the entry of
Bruce Wasserstein into Lazard Frères in 2002 precipitated the firm's
going public in 2005, after 157 years of private ownership. In the
latter case, a change in the identity of ownership brought out differences in the partners' visions for the future of the firm that could
only be resolved through a change of ownership form. On the other
hand, there are also many cases in which a change in the identity of
ownership does not affect strategy, such as when a son or daughter
carries on the family business along the same lines as the father and

mother, or when, as in the case of Pictet, a new owner-partner is chosen with continuity in mind.

If we compare the cases of Pictet and Lazard Frères (prior to 2005), the importance of considering the values of the newly chosen partners is clearly apparent. While both firms look(ed) for partners who would be vocal in shaping the future of the firm, Pictet insists on loyalty – according to de Saussure, this is precisely the reason why the firm did not offer a partnership to anyone outside a narrow circle of Geneva families the last time a new partner was chosen (in 2009): "although there were candidates from outside, we worried that choosing such a person might be misunderstood as a move towards eventually selling the firm." Lazard Frères, by contrast, had evolved into a form of mixed ownership with "capitalists," most of whom were silent but some, like Michel David-Weill, were very vocal and "working partners" who themselves were divided according to value: internal (continuity of the firm) vs. external (return on investment relative to the market). In this explosive mixture, the election of new partner Wasserstein to the position of CEO and the deal-focused people he subsequently brought in tipped the balance in favor of the activists who wanted to maximize their return on investment.[11]

The case of Lazard Frères highlights the fact that several different types of shareholders can be present, even in privately held firms. Thus, it is not uncommon for family firms, particularly as they grow older and include younger generations, to include both entrepreneur and sleeper shareholders. In fact, one of the key issues in the governance of family-owned firms concerns the sleepers: to what extent and in what manner should shareholders who are not active in the running of the firm be allowed to participate in decisions concerning changes of strategy and decisions concerning changes of ownership?[12] Even thornier problems present themselves when traders and activists looking for an exit try to coexist with entrepreneurs and sleepers in privately held firms: in these situations a buyout of some sort often is the only way to avoid endless disagreements over how to lead the firm, an IPO in the case of Lazard Frères or a sale of shares from traders and activists to entrepreneurs and sleepers for many family firms.

Point to watch: resolving shareholder differences

It is not always possible to resolve differences among shareholders. In some cases, these differences can be so severe as to block needed change in the firm for many years (see Chapter 6). Short of trying to ensure that all shareholders share the same values as Pictet does by explicitly incorporating this consideration in their choice of new partners, a private firm with say over who its shareholders are can set up a series of hurdles for attaining shareholder status: length of service, level of commitment, and extent of contribution, for example. However, it is equally important to recognize that the personal conditions as well as the perspectives of shareholders can change over time and to therefore provide for a fair means and price of exit, so that decision-making is not blocked if shareholders become irreconcilably opposed.

In the publicly listed firm, the shareholder roster fluctuates continuously. Most of the fluctuation happens within the category of traders, shareholders who have an external value (the market) and do not make any direct effort to actively influence the strategy of the firm. The power they do have stems from the implicit threat of sale: if dissatisfied with strategy or performance they may sell, leading to a fall in the share price and, ultimately, an increase in the cost of capital of the firm.[13] For this reason, managers pay careful attention to satisfying the expectations of traders, and this is what primarily distinguishes publicly listed firms from privately held firms in the analysis of changes in the identity of ownership. Changes in the ranks of entrepreneurs and sleepers, as well as movements of activists are more rare, but, as in the case of privately held firms, typically signal major changes.

Privately held firm: new shareholders – new strategy?

In the privately held firm, the entry of new shareholders constitutes a rare and major change event – it needs to be prepared very conscientiously. What questions should decision-makers be asking of new shareholders? In the privately held firm, the family firm or the partnership, there are usually no traders to be concerned about, but new shareholders can still be of three types: activists, owners, or sleepers. When considering potential new shareholders, the first point to ascertain is the shareholder type. In some cases, such as the passing of the baton of ownership and management in the family firm, the shareholder type (entrepreneur) is given; in other cases, like that of Pictet that explicitly seeks entrepreneurs and does not want activists as partners, analysis of the type represented by a prospective shareholder requires considerably more time and effort.

By definition, new entrepreneurs and new activists will demand a voice in the running of the firm. In family firms and most partnerships, insiders are required to build up a track record before they accede to ownership, and their track record should provide ample indication of the strategic choices they are likely to support. This is why ownership change often does not imply strategy change in the privately held firm. As the story of Lazard Frères shows, much more care is required where outsiders are invited in to the firm, whether as family members, partners, or merely as providers of capital. In effect, the case of the changing of the guard at Seagram alluded to earlier also falls into the outsider category, because Edgar Bronfman came to the firm after years of dabbling in the movie industry and did not have a deep connection with the core business of the firm. Inasmuch as outsiders are often brought in to make strategy changes, the relationship between change in the identity of ownership and change of strategy is not surprising or unwanted.

The analysis becomes more complicated when shareholders turn out not to be what they seem or simply evolve: a new shareholder who professes not to have any intention to exit may still turn out to be an activist looking to sell; a shareholder who is initially content to be a sleeper may respond to changed circumstances in the firm by demanding a voice. The bottom line is that the privately held firm should exercise a great deal of caution in choosing new shareholders. Many do, but for those who don't, the stories of Seagram and Lazard Frères ought to serve as reminders of what can happen to strategy when ownership changes in an uncontrolled manner.

Publicly listed firm: new shareholders – old strategy?

Compared to the privately held firm, the publicly listed firm experiences much more frequent turnover of shareholders. Most of this turnover can be attributed to traders who hold the shares of the firm for relatively short periods of time and do not seek to actively influence decision-making. The principal weapon of the trader in interacting with the firm is the threat of sale. Although traders all share the intention to exit, they differ among themselves in their motivations for holding any particular share. Thus, a large NYSE index firm like JP Morgan or Pfizer is likely to have at least two different types of traders on its shareholding roster: (a) those who hold the share in their portfolio based on the risk of stocks in the portfolio[14] and (b) those who hold the share in their portfolio because its prospects correspond to the portfolio's particular objectives: i.e., growth or value. Both of these types of traders, through the implicit threat of sale, place expectations on the management of the firm, but their expectations are not the same.[15] In the case of a firm like JP Morgan, for example, the portfolio risk-based trader looks for steady results (so as not to affect the level of risk in the portfolio), whereas the trader with a theme of rapid profit growth wants the firm to take on more risk.

Even to satisfy the different expectations of diverse traders, in other words, management is forced to make difficult choices. Of course, management does not react to every change in the shareholder roster, but there is considerable evidence to suggest that the management of publicly listed firms does pay careful attention to the wishes of traders.[16] More generally, we can say that in many firms, the litany of quarterly reports, investor conferences, and statements to the press that is required of the publicly listed firm puts a lot of pressure on management to adapt strategy to the wishes of those traders who are quickest to pull the trigger.

This can, in turn, lead management to follow fashion: globalize at all costs, jump on the internet bandwagon, or play the easy credit game, to name the leading fashions of the last ten years.[17] Rare are the publicly listed firms that can resist the implicit threat to sell that backs the pressure applied by traders (unless, of course, the firm has a committed core ownership of entrepreneurs and sleepers that protects it from having to satisfy short-term market expectations). Those that do successfully resist are typically very large (making them an essential part of index holdings and hence dangerous to leave out of any portfolio measured against the index) and have a strong and long track record of meeting their earnings targets. A prototypical example is Nestlé, a firm that constitutes over 20 percent of the SMI (Swiss Market Index) and, for over twenty years now (since the years under Helmut Maucher's leadership in the 1990s) has refused to satisfy analyst demands for quarterly figures and repeatedly made unpopular decisions on its path to slow, but steady profit growth. Among publicly listed firms with a broadly dispersed shareholding structure, firms like Nestlé (or Johnson & Johnson in the USA) that can go against market expectations are the exception that proves the rule. The movements of traders are very much on the minds of the managers of most publicly listed firms and have a definite impact on decision-making and strategic choices.

The entry of activists in the publicly listed firm

We have already remarked that the presence of traders is one of the key distinguishing characteristics of publicly listed firms, as compared to privately held firms. Activists can exist in both forms of ownership, but are more common in the publicly listed firm (privately held firms usually choose to keep all externally oriented shareholders out of ownership, unless they cannot do otherwise or are mistakenly convinced that an activist is an entrepreneur, as in the case of Lazard Frères).

Among publicly listed firms, there are those that flout the expectations of traders despite poor track records, holding on to strategies, capital structures, and governance arrangements that go against "what markets want." This is the kind of firm that may sooner or later become the target of activists, shareholders who typically take minority positions, attempt to bring about clearly defined changes, and sell their shares once the changes have been made (and market appreciation of the changes has caused the share price to go up).[18] Prominent recent examples of companies targeted by activists include Infineon in Germany, Accor in France, Shell in the United Kingdom, and Time Warner in the United States, but a full list would also include many less well-known mid caps and be very long.

Activists come in many shapes – pension funds, investment funds, and hedge funds, to name the most common forms – and do not all operate with the same time horizon or follow the exact same recipe for effecting change. In general, however, activists are all looking for the same kind of opportunity to invest, that is to say a firm that has significantly underperformed its peers for some time in terms of share price development, but has a strong set of core assets that could be more effectively employed, if incumbent management were persuaded to do so or simply removed and replaced by a more astute management team. The underperformance of firms that become the targets of activists like the Hermes Focus Funds, Colony Capital, or Icahn typically can be traced to one or more of the following characteristics:

• Strategy: unrelated diversification and/or failed internationalization;
• Capital Structure: insufficient leverage and/or excess cash position;
• Governance: powerless board and/or weak shareholder rights.

Firms that display these characteristics and underperform their peers for any length of time discourage traders. Activists thus benefit from a low share price at entry and, because they do not seek to take over the firm, do not pay the premium for control. In effect, activists seek to induce changes without control, by working with the board and management, by gaining the critical support of entrepreneurs and sleepers (especially in cases where there are significant sleepers) and traders, and by selectively applying the pressure of the media. Activists do not always succeed in bringing about the changes they are pushing, but when they do, and this can take several years, the market recognizes what has been achieved and comes streaming back into the stock that it had previously given up on. This signals the time for activists, who are not entrepreneurs in the sense defined earlier, to exit. The firm has made changes to strategy, capital structure, and governance, the share price has risen, and the work of the activist is done.

Point to watch: under constant scrutiny

Publicly listed firms are under constant scrutiny, not just by traders who are ready to buy or sell at any instant, but also by activists who are looking for the right opportunity and the right time to get involved. With the increasing prevalence of activists, many American and European firms have moved to protect themselves by taking preemptive action: it is much easier (and safer) for managers to unwind corporate strategies of unrelated diversification and return excess cash of their own accord, than to wait until activists impel them to do so. As a result of this pressure to conform to what activists and the financial markets in general consider to be good strategy, there is today less variety in the corporate landscape. Whether this is always good for the firms concerned or indeed for the economy as a whole remains to be seen.

In the publicly listed firm, the arrival of either new activists or new traders can signal that a change of strategy is on the table. Although shareholders in the publicly listed firm generally cannot change strategy as directly or quickly as shareholders in the privately held firm, it is not true to assert that there is no relationship between ownership and strategy in the publicly listed firm. The relationship exists, but it is complex, different types of shareholders play different roles, and an eventual change in strategy becomes a matter of influence and negotiation among shareholders and management. In general, the effect of changes in the identity of ownership on strategy takes time to manifest itself; anywhere from a few months in the case of firms forced to withdraw particular proposals under shareholder pressure to several years in the case of firms pushed to make asset sales in order to satisfy shareholder demands.

Point to watch: activists' new lines of attack

Themselves under pressure from investors for higher returns and running out of easy targets as more firms adapt their strategy, capital structure, and corporate governance to deflect the attention of potential activists, an increasing number of activists are turning to more specialized lines of attack. Thus, there are now activists specialized in financial services or activists specialized in oil and gas. These new activists are characterized by deep industry knowledge and a focus on improving how businesses are run. Olivant Advisors, for example, suggests that, in financial services, it is able to create "fundamental change through operational improvements" (www.olivant.com/strategy). Not surprisingly, activists of this more specialized type are staffed by industry experts and led by individuals with senior executive experience in the industry. In cases where these activists get involved, the traditional lines between ownership, management, and strategy are thoroughly blurred.

The entry of new entrepreneurs and new sleepers in the publicly listed firm

For the publicly listed firm like for the privately held firm, the entry of a new entrepreneur or a new sleeper is a rare event, but it does happen, if only under special circumstances. Thus, in the case of Swiss industrial concern Oerlikon OC, for example, the existing owner, the Anda-Bührle founder family, had evolved into a sleeper and wanted to liquidate its holdings. This provided the occasion for Austrian activists Pecik and Stumpf (Victory Holding) to buy a large stake that they then sold on to the Renova group of Viktor Vekselberg who, in turn, has emphasized that they are entrepreneurs who will be around for a long time and take a strong interest in shaping the strategy of the firm. In the case of German travel concern TUI, described above, the management of the firm invited the Moroccan state to take stakes; the Moroccans obliged and, as model sleepers, have faithfully supported the decisions of management ever since, even against very vocal activists. In general, new entrepreneurs or new sleepers without a previous relationship to the firm only come in at the invitation of decision-makers (existing shareholders or management) in the firm.

As defined, new entrepreneur and new sleeper shareholders will have other interests besides maximizing the share price (internal values), and these interests are likely to affect the strategy of the firm, at least where the strategy and the interests of the new shareholders come into contact. The Renova group of Viktor Vekselberg, for example, is using Oerlikon OC to pursue a technology development strategy that may or may not pay off for the other shareholders of the firm. The Moroccan state has acquired shares in TUI primarily to ensure continued German tourist business for Moroccan travel destinations. In considering whether to offer shares to new entrepreneurs or new sleepers, decision-makers therefore need to carefully think through the long-term implications. Long-term ownership engagements should not overlook the fact that the situation of the new shareholders may also change. Thus, sovereign wealth funds such as Singapore's GIC or Qatar's Investment Authority may be brought on board today as sleepers, but no one knows whether or not they will one day become vocal, especially if a firm loses money consistently and has to be bailed out or if a firm pursues a strategy that runs counter to the interests (internal values) of the sovereign wealth fund's stakeholders.[19]

Same shareholders, changing types

Even though shareholders may be initially identified as representing a particular type, their type is not forever fixed: entrepreneurs, like founder families and state organizations, may lose influence or lose interest and become sleepers; sleepers like sovereign wealth funds may be forced by their own stakeholders to wake up and take a more vocal stance. Similarly, an activist can start to act like a trader, disengaging from the company and looking for the best time to sell, and a trader can become vocal, joining forces with activists to force a firm with a poor record to make strategy changes. Although they do not show up in the shareholder roster, these are also important change events in the identity of ownership with corresponding effects on management and strategy.

When shareholders change character in this manner, it is either because the shareholders themselves have evolved or because the shareholding in the firm is no longer meeting their objectives. Although this kind of change is also rare and does not happen overnight, no firm can rely on shareholder stability. At Japanese advertising giant Dentsu, for example, traders and sleepers had quietly accepted years of strategic indecision and mediocre results. Only in 2009, a full eight years after the firm's IPO, did the *same* shareholders reach the breaking point and join forces, getting management to commit to a new strategy of aggressive global expansion.[20] In order to understand why and how strategic decisions are made in publicly listed companies, one has to analyze the evolution of shareholders. Shareholder rosters change, and shareholders themselves can also change. Too much management attention may be focused on short-term movements in share price that do not have strategic implications. The real action having a lasting effect on strategy is elsewhere. A change in the identity of ownership, by numbers or by type, is the kind of signal that decision-makers need to pay particular attention to, if they want to keep the firm on course.

III. Shifts in the balance of forces among shareholders

The vast majority of firms, in terms of number, have a single shareholder or a close-knit (typically family) group of shareholders. If one restricts the analysis to the smaller circle of larger firms, however, we find that many firms have a *mix* of different types of shareholders, entrepreneurs, sleepers, activists, and, in the case of publicly listed firms, traders. In these firms, the influence of ownership on strategy depends on how the mix of shareholders interacts with nonshareholder management. By the weight of their shareholdings or by persuasion, alone or in coalition with others, shareholders make their views known and try to affect the direction of the firm.

When diverse shareholders with different values and different methods confront diverse executives who, as we shall describe in Chapter 2, have their own values and their own methods, strategy choices result from the emergence of dominant coalitions between diverse shareholders and diverse executives. Thus, a change in the identity of ownership just as much as a change in the identity of the chief executive and his/her team can lead to a reconsideration of strategy. Shareholder influence on strategy can change as new types of shareholders enter the mix (see above) or if there is a shift in the balance of forces among existing shareholders. Both in privately held firms and in publicly listed firms, there are distinctive shifts in the balance of shareholders to watch for. Unlike the entry of new types of shareholders, these shifts take place over time and are therefore harder to pinpoint and react to.

Shifts in the balance of forces among shareholders of privately held firms

In the privately held firm, most notably the family firm and the partnership, the most problematic shift in the balance among shareholders to watch for is the shift from sleepers to activists. With the passing of generations in the family firm, the likelihood grows that some family shareholders will not wish (or have the ability) to carry on the tradition of entrepreneur shareholding. These family members may act as sleepers for some time, but, eventually, there is a danger that they start looking for a way to exit (i.e., adopt external values). If they do not represent a significant percentage of the shareholding body, they can be bought out (as frequently happens), but if the sleepers adopting external values become a majority and desire to actively influence the direction of the firm as activists, the strategy will be affected. Family shareholders acting as activists will seek to prevent major new investments and try to focus attention on making the firm easier to sell: disentangling the assets and cleaning up the books.

> ### Point to watch: preparing for transitions in the family firm
>
> Many family firms put off making arrangements for a generational transition for too long. Founders, in particular, have trouble imagining what the firm might look like without them. At a minimum, decision-makers need to think about the different roles family members will play in the business, as owners and, perhaps, also as board members and/or executives. Recognizing that the values and methods of family members may change over time and that younger generations are unlikely to all have the same values and methods as the founding generation, it is important to put in place a process whereby each successive generation can reexamine their place in the firm and their agreement on the governance principles of the firm. No governance framework should be cast in stone, but rather should be adapted to the changing contexts of the business and its shareholders.

In order to nip this kind of shift of the balance of forces in the family firm in the bud, it is necessary to offer erstwhile sleepers a way out, a means for establishing a fair price for exiting. A public offering provides such a means, but at the price of a loss of freedom for those family members who want to stay and pursue an active role as entrepreneur shareholders. A less strategically constraining means of obtaining the capital for a buyout is to invite in a select group of shareholders who accept well-defined terms of engagement and a clear timeline for exit. In recent years, a small industry has grown up around family firms investing in other family firms in this manner. The key for decision-makers in family firms is to recognize that family members can develop different interests over time and to be ready to help family members to exit the shareholding of the family firm when (if not before) they wish to do so.

As illustrated in the descriptions of Pictet and Lazard, every new partner is a potential threat to the balance of forces in the partnership. Even among existing partners, however, time can bring significant changes in outlook. Partners who have been around for many years may become more interested in selling the firm (this is what happened in the case of KPMG Consulting to be described in Chapter 3) and start to think like activists and traders rather than like entrepreneurs. Again, it is important to anticipate this kind of generational shift with clearly set-out rules and terms for exit. At Pictet, for example, a written partnership agreement states that retiring partners exit at book value. Of course, not all changes in the balance of forces among shareholders can be predicted or dealt with by contracts. Sometimes the personal circumstances of some partners evolve away from involvement in the firm; sometimes the business environment is such that exit starts to look especially attractive to some. No family and certainly no partnership should ever assume that the values of shareholders stay the same.

Shifts in the balance of forces among shareholders of publicly listed firms

In the publicly listed firm, shifts in the balance of forces among shareholders can occur in a variety of ways. Even without the entry of new shareholders, erstwhile entrepreneurs can evolve into sleepers (see the example of Oerlikon OC cited earlier), sleepers can become vocal, and even traders can decide to speak up and take action on issues of special interest. Changes in the character of existing shareholders, in turn, can tip the balance on questions of major strategic significance. Activists, in particular, will often try very hard to win traders over to their cause, so as to be able to exert more pressure on management to make changes to governance and strategy. In some cases, the struggle for shareholder support can resemble the scramble for votes on divisive issues in parliamentary government.

Consider the example of the Swiss bank, UBS. UBS is a large and very well-established name in banking with the biggest private banking franchise in the world (in terms of assets under management); these characteristics make it a prime choice for sleepers seeking the stable and risk-free returns of wealth management. At the same time, UBS also has a significant investment bank, actively involved in all kinds of very volatile trading activities; this makes it a prime choice for traders seeking the explosive profit growth and volatility that the trading results of investment banking can provide. Clearly the interests of the first kind of shareholder and the second kind of shareholder do not coincide. From the perspective of Berle and Means, this is precisely the kind of dispersed shareholding that permits management to make strategic choices independent of shareholder preferences.

However, in the publicly listed firm of today, management is not just an employee, but also a (sometimes significant) shareholder.[21] In this situation, it is clear that management plays an important role in the balance among shareholders. In effect, management can tilt strategy in the direction of the preference of one type of shareholder and against the preferences of other types. This is what happened in the cases of UBS and a number of other publicly traded banks with a similar mix of stable and risky activities (i.e., Deutsche Bank, Citibank, etc.). By promising very high levels of return on equity, the management of these banks effectively took sides, with shareholders seeking profit growth and against shareholders seeking stable dividends.[22]

> **Point to watch: when management takes sides**
> When the management of a publicly listed firm states that decisions are being taken in the interest of shareholder value, it is

important to pinpoint whom they have in mind. Arguably, many decisions defended as shareholder value driven are aimed at generating share price increases in the short term. As such, these decisions may increase the level of risk borne by the firm and therefore ultimately endanger shareholders who have no intention of selling, such as entrepreneurs and sleepers. Interestingly, even in firms with large shareholders, management may focus on attracting traders to the share. By doing so, managers are in effect siding with traders: the closer their own incentives are aligned to the short-term development of the share price, the more likely managers are to make such a "deal with the devil."

Change in the identity of ownership – conclusion

Shareholders stand for confidence in the firm and represent stability. If the shareholding body itself becomes unstable, the future direction of the firm is called into question. We have differentiated between two different types of changes in the identity of ownership: an entry of new shareholders and a shift in the balance of forces among existing shareholders. In either case, it is critical for decision-makers in the firm to understand the values and the methods of the different shareholders. The interaction of these different shareholder perspectives with the point of view of executive management ultimately determines the strategy of the firm.

TWO

Change in management

The executive defines strategies and implements operational decisions to direct the company, within the framework of the powers granted by shareholders and the board of directors. Instances of executive succession therefore represent a prime opportunity for ownership to confirm the adopted course or to set new strategic priorities.[1] However, it is wrong to regard the executive as a mere instrument of ownership. In some cases of executive succession, such as where a new executive is put in place by shareholders seeking strategic change (i.e., private equity), he or she does indeed stick very closely to the designs of ownership. Generally, however, it is more accurate to think of the new executive as an independent actor whose ability to make things happen depends upon his/her relationship with shareholders and the board of directors.[2]

When does a firm experience a change in management? In the case of a firm that is performing to the satisfaction of its shareholders and where there is broad agreement over strategy, the question of executive succession arises in the context of passing the torch, from one generation of leadership to the next: age or other interests prompt the current executive to step down. Although this process is never easy, it is rarely explicitly concerned with strategy, except in stressing continuity. Where the firm is in danger or where there is substantial disagreement in the ownership over strategy, on the other hand, executive succession represents the chance for a real break with the past and is very much concerned with strategy. The focus is on choosing an executive who will find a new way to get the firm on track again.[3]

In light of the principal contexts of executive succession, a passing of the torch or a need for a new way, it is not surprising that much of the debate about succession in nomination committees centers on the insider vs. outsider question.[4] An insider to the firm is supposed to be ideal for continuing along the established path, while an outsider is commonly considered to be the better choice for revamping the firm and pursuing a new direction. Focusing on whether a candidate for executive succession is an insider or an outsider opens the door to two kinds of errors: first, decision-makers may have wrongly assessed the context, assuming that all is well, when dark clouds are already on the horizon; in this situation the insider vs. outsider question is the wrong starting point for the executive succession debate; and, second, hiring an insider (or an outsider) for the top job gives a false sense of security; some insiders, put in place to stay the course, in fact pursue major change, while some outsiders, chosen to lead change, turn out to want to stick to established practices or are stifled by the organization and fail to make a difference.[5]

Rather than focusing on the insider vs. outsider question, we have found it more useful to consider executive succession in light of a careful analysis of the context of the firm and in view of the potential successors' values and methods. Starting with an accurate appraisal of the context of the firm, decision-makers (typically the board of directors) need to ask themselves what kind of leadership is needed going forward: a leadership that is likely to stay the course or a leadership that is likely to pursue major change. The question of whether executives can be categorized in terms of their method has received considerable research attention. What this work has shown is that executives can be characterized in terms of how they approach change. Thus, whereas some executives generally act to maintain continuity, others are not content with the status quo and habitually seek a rupture with the past. Table 2.1 below provides examples of typical continuity and rupture-driven initiatives.[6]

TABLE 2.1 *Executive succession: methods*

Methods	
Rupture	Continuity
- *Develop new strategy*	- *Stay the course*
- *Change systems, rewards*	- *Make process improvements*
- *Bring in new people, new ways*	- *Follow industry best practices*

Continuity-oriented executives and rupture-oriented executives can be further differentiated according to their values. There are continuity-oriented executives who stick to the established way of doing things in the firm and continuity-oriented executives who take best practice in the profession or the industry as a guide, working to make the firm as good as the standard, but not questioning the standard. The difference between these two types of continuity-oriented executives lies in their values, internal for the executive who maintains the company way, external for the executive who relies on external standards of best practice. Rupture-oriented executives also differ according to their values. There is the externally anchored executive who follows the expectations of the market – whatever is currently "in" with investors or consultants (as the makers of external standards) gets this type of executive's attention and orients his/her change initiatives. The executive inclined towards rupture who adheres to internal values, by contrast, bases his/her approach on a logic that is specific to the firm – its tradition, its people, and its skills. The different values to consider in executive succession are summarized in Table 2.2.[7]

Like in the case of diverse shareholders discussed in Chapter 1, we can now classify executives according to methods and values. Again, we find four distinct categories: *technocrats* who seek

TABLE 2.2 *Executive succession: values*

	External	- Equity market demands - Industry standards
Values		
	Internal	- Specific to the firm - Firm tradition

continuity and subscribe to external values such as functional standards of best practice; *adopters* who are inclined towards rupture, but also subscribe to external values, as exemplified by executives who aim to give "the markets" the strategy story they want; *transformers* who also seek rupture, but subscribe to internal values specific to the firm; and *custodians* who are inclined towards continuity, but also subscribe to internal values, as exemplified by executives who preserve the status quo and maintain the existing values of the firm. The four categories of executive are set out in Table 2.3 and will be referred to henceforth in discussing differences among executives.

TABLE 2.3 *Executive succession: values and methods*

		Methods	
		Rupture	Continuity
Values	External	- Adopter	- Technocrat
	Internal	- Transformer	- Custodian

In the news media, transformers and adopters seeking rupture attract the most attention, and many of the best-known executives fall into one or the other of these two categories. Thus, Steve Jobs and Jack Welch are very good examples of transformers who built on the existing values of their firms to revolutionize the competitive landscape of an industry (in the case of Jobs at Apple, the firm he himself created) and change the meaning of corporate strategy (in the case of Welch at GE). Contrast the actions of Jobs and Welch with those of Jean-Marie Messier at Vivendi Universal and Jürgen

Schrempp at DaimlerChrysler: Messier turned the once staid utility Vivendi into a media giant in the late 1990s, in order to attract the attention of trader shareholders seeking internet growth stories and bolster his own reputation as an architect of change; Schrempp merged Daimler with the incompatible Chrysler and created what became known as the "Welt AG" (World, Inc.), with the intention of making DaimlerChrysler the most global player in its industry. Whereas Jobs and Welch drove change in recognition of what made their own firms unique, Messier and Schrempp justified their ruptures with the past in terms of external values.[8]

Technocrats share an external value orientation with adopters. However, where adopters try to make prevailing market trends their own, technocrats look for improvements in the basics of the value chain – purchasing, manufacturing, and distribution logistics, but also cash management and human resource processes. The technocrat stresses measurable progress over grand designs, and his/her public pronouncements emphasize raising the performance of the firm to the level of the industry or the professional standard. In practice, technocrats often succeed transformers or adopters, because decision-makers (i.e., boards of directors choosing the next executive) recognize that periods of rupture can leave a firm vulnerable to capability deficits. Thus, we have Jeffrey Immelt following Jack Welch at GE, or John Reed succeeding the visionary Walter Wriston at Citibank. Whereas technocrats conceive of change relative to external standards of best practice, custodians like to leave things as they are. In many cases, custodian executives are put in place by a dominant shareholder to guarantee continuity; alternatively, when a retiring CEO moves on to become chairperson of the board of directors, he/she may lobby to put a custodian in place to maintain the strategic trajectory of the firm. Either way, custodians are not likely to attract a great deal of attention from the markets or the media.

For the sake of simplifying, we have spoken of the executive in the singular, as if senior management were one person. While this may be accurate in the specific case of executive succession, where the firm is looking for one person to take the helm, it is not a realistic approximation of any senior management team. The CEO, then, may be a custodian or a transformer, but the senior management team is unlikely to be composed entirely of the same category of executives, unless the whole team has been replaced in one stroke. In a senior management team that has grown over years, different types will coexist, an adopter as CEO with a technocrat as CFO and a custodian as COO, for example. Clearly, the coexistence of executives with differing, perhaps even opposite values and methods, bears the potential for considerable conflict over strategy and the direction of the firm.[9] Unless one has analyzed the composition of the senior management team, one cannot say which strategy the executive group is going to advocate. We will return to this question in Chapter 4, when we look at the reasons for and impact of reorganization, and in Chapters 6 and 7, when we take a closer look at situations in which decision-making is blocked. For the rest of this chapter, however, we focus on executive succession and the role of the CEO in driving changes in strategy and triggering changes in ownership and governance.

I. Change in the identity of management – change in strategy

The values and methods of senior managers differ and have a decisive influence on how the executive conceives of and carries out the job. How can a potential CEO's value and method be determined? Clearly, the search for a new executive has to start a definition of the skills that are necessary for the job – business skills, leadership skills, and relational skills. Depending on the specifics of the job and the context of succession, the weighting of these skills may differ, of course, and some situations may require a preponderance of special skills such as turnaround management or market development or cost control. A firm in need of a turnaround looks for an executive with a track record of successful turnarounds. The track record, and the breadth of relevant experience of the potential successor, give him or her the legitimacy to take on the new challenge.[10]

Does past experience help predict if a new executive will actually meet the expectations of decision-makers and act as a worthy heir (continuity) or be the change agent (rupture) the firm needs? To some extent, yes: with Carlos Ghosn's past as a highly successful turnaround manager fresh on everyone's mind, no one at Renault could possibly have expected him to leave things the way they were under Louis Schweitzer when he succeeded Schweitzer at the helm of Renault in 2005. Similarly, Franklin Raines' background as a former general partner at sophisticated Lazard Frères should have given decision-makers at Fannie Mae some indication that although Raines was coming to the job from a government post at the Office of Management and Budget (OMB), he would not be content to let the lender be a simple lender and would instead be likely to take the organization into more complex and more risky areas of business – as he did, a strategy that eventually led to a very large government bailout.

In other cases, the relationship between an executive's past experience and his/her perspective on change is less clear-cut, particularly if the executive has not made a name for himself/herself leading significant change efforts. A successor from inside a family or other close-knit ownership group may take the long-awaited opportunity of the executive appointment to try to finally make a mark; an outside successor known for a continuity-oriented approach to change may find the environment of the new firm gives him or her the longed for chance to do something new and exciting. Clearly, past experience can only be a rough guide to understanding how executive succession will impact firm strategy.[11]

Point to watch: past may not predict future behavior

A particularly challenging situation arises when managers take on an executive position in a new firm with a different form of ownership from what they are used to, i.e., changing from publicly listed to private, or from government controlled to publicly listed. In cases such as these, managers are confronted not only with a new management brief, but also with a new governance context, and this can lead to unexpected complications. Thus, the family firm that brings in a new CEO from a listed company to give it more operational discipline (as a technocrat) may find that the new executive is just as interested in adopting the performance metrics and strategic objectives of the financial markets (as an adopter). In general, executives do not adjust to changes in ownership form easily and need to be specifically coached to function in the new governance context.

Another way to look at the problem of executive succession and to get at the question of the values of the candidate is to consider the executive not just as a manager and leader, but also as a shareholder. In the canon of finance, shareholders are shareholders and managers are managers, but in today's reality executives are very often also important shareholders, or, if not formally shareholders (i.e., the nonfamily executive in the family-owned firm), then in some way incentivized like shareholders. Thus, the job of the executive is not just a job with a salary, but also a financial investment. A great deal has been said about the financial incentives given to executives, fixed or variable, short-term or long-term, to align their motivation with the objectives of the firm.[12] A lot less has been written about the investment time horizon of the executive.[13] Does the executive see the job as a long-term commitment to a joint future or as a short-term engagement, to be milked for all it is worth, and then traded in for another executive position somewhere else? Past history is an indication here too, of course, but so is age, financial position, and cupidity.[14] Not all executives view financial incentives in the same way, so finding the "right" financial incentives cannot be the answer to all questions of executive motivation. Some executives, transformers, and custodians with internal values, will be predisposed to view their appointment as a long-term ownership proposition, while others will behave more like shareholders who eventually intend to sell. The executive who behaves like a shareholder preparing to sell is likely to try to make one (or more) major move(s) to render the firm more attractive to prospective buyers during his or her tenure, either strategic in the case of the adopter or operational in the case of the technocrat, in order to make the most of the investment.[15]

Point to watch: time horizon of the executive

Viewing new executives as potential shareholders highlights the link between the executives' values and methods and their time horizons. In accepting a new position, an executive is making an investment – in their development as a manager, of course, but just as importantly, in their career payoff. As such, the executive will be looking at the new position as a step in a series of payoffs. Depending on how the executive views their career progression, it may be the time to roll the dice and take a big bet (with the company's money) or it may be the time to collect dividends. In considering these questions, the board of directors should not forget that the time horizon of the executive also depends on the state of the market for executives and structure incentive compensation accordingly.

In summary, we can say that executives who act as transformers or adopters will seek to change the strategy of the firm during their tenure. Technocrats and custodians, on the other hand, will stick to the existing strategy, either looking for operational improvements (technocrats) or just following the established trajectory (custodians). From the point of view of those charged with overseeing executive succession, it is important to be able to make a valid assessment of the candidates' methods and values prior to deciding who gets the job. We have argued that the candidates' past records only tell part of the story and that an analysis of the record needs to be supplemented with an evaluation of the executive as a potential shareholder.

II. Change in the identity of management – change in ownership

If we accept the argument that a candidate for executive succession may view their appointment in shareholder terms, then it is clear that a change in management cannot be considered in isolation from questions of ownership. Indeed, executive succession can be the first step in a change of ownership form, or, less dramatically, in a change in the identity of ownership. For example, a new executive can work to take a publicly listed firm private (management buyout, or MBO), either alone, or in partnership with other managers and shareholders (often private equity). Similarly, a new executive can focus his or her efforts on preparing the firm for sale to a third party (arguably, this is what Bruce Wasserstein did at Lazard Frères, in the case highlighted in Chapter 1). This scenario can also apply to family-owned firms, even where the new executive is a family member; the new family executive may see the firm more as an activist than as an entrepreneur, and decide that his/her personal (or the family's) financial assets are better invested somewhere else. We do not mean to imply that MBOs and sales to third parties happen without the input of existing shareholders, but merely wish to point out that a change in management can lead to a change in ownership and therefore should be an occasion for existing shareholders to reflect on their plans for continued ownership. When choosing a successor for the executive office, every firm needs to think about the implications of executive succession for ownership.[16]

Even when a change in management does not lead to a change in ownership form, it can still have profound effects on the identity of ownership. In the family firm or the closely held firm, the advent of new management can lead to a concentration of the shareholding structure as certain members of the family decide to sell their shares, either because they are asked to do so by the new family executive or because they do not wish to follow the new leader. In the publicly listed firm, a new executive can attract new shareholders who are convinced to invest by the track record and strategy of the new management and, at the same time, turn away existing shareholders who are not willing to go along with the new team's approach. The merger of the Swiss Banking Corporation and the Union Bank of Switzerland to form UBS in 1998 and the subsequent appointment of Marcel Ospel to the position of CEO (chairman from 2001 to 2008), for example, led to the adoption of a strategy weighted towards the volatile earnings of investment banking and attracted many new speculative funds to the UBS share; where before they had shunned the stock as staid, these funds now cheered the new adopter executive on to taking ever greater risks. Today, once again under new management and ostensibly rededicated to the core businesses of private banking and wealth management (with a smaller investment banking arm), UBS is less attractive to speculative funds.[17]

Point to watch: alliances of the new executive

Every new CEO has to pass muster with shareholders, either before taking on the job in the case of firms with entrepreneurs and/or influential activists in the shareholding body (such as family firms and partnerships, for example), or once appointed by the board in the case of publicly listed firms dominated by traders and sleepers.

In either context, the new CEO begins his/her job by establishing working relationships with key shareholder representatives. These relationships may start out in a neutral manner, but can blossom into alliances, with the CEO drawing on the support of some shareholders to overcome the resistance of others opposed to his/her policies. In other words, different shareholders will try to co-opt the CEO, and the CEO, in turn, will look for allies in the shareholding body.

III. Change in the identity of management – change in governance

If the nomination of a new chief executive can lead to changes in the strategy of the firm and, in some cases, also to changes in the ownership of the firm, it is clear that the governance systems of the firm can also be affected by executive succession. The governance systems of the firm, the structures and processes that specify how decisions are made and who is accountable, are not cast in stone, but, rather, evolve with the context. A change in management can affect governance systems in at least three ways: (a) the choice of a new chief executive may reveal weaknesses in the executive selection process, leading shareholders and board members to rethink that process; (b) the strategy pursued by a new chief executive may involve the firm in new risks that require approaches to measurement and control that differ significantly from those already in place; and (c) the new chief executive may accumulate a great deal of power over decision-making in the firm, effectively making it necessary, at some point, for shareholders and board members to reassert themselves and reclaim their original roles in the governance of the firm. Let us now look at each of these three changes in governance induced by changes in management in more detail.

Rethinking the executive selection process

In many family-owned and closely held firms, there is no formal executive selection process in place. The next (qualified) person in line from the family or the group inherits the top job. This works as long as there are no major disturbances: if the executive selection process is contested or if the heir apparent does not pan out, the firm is thrown into turmoil. This is what happened a few years ago at family-owned travel service giant Carlson Companies, Inc., when Marilyn Carlson-Nelson (who owns 50 percent of the shares of the company her father founded and controls all of the voting rights) stepped down from the top job, to let her son, Curtis Carlson, Jr., take the reins. Although company governance guidelines specified that the chairman/CEO had to be a family member and Curtis Carlson, Jr. was the only candidate from the family, the initiatives he launched met with such strong opposition inside the firm that he had to be removed, after only a few months at the helm. As a result, and in the absence of another family candidate, the firm was forced to adapt its governance: Marilyn Carlson-Nelson would come back in the role of chair, but, for the first time in the history of the firm, an external search firm was hired and a nonfamily CEO was appointed (Hubert Joly).[18]

Ultimately, corporate governance is concerned with who directs the firm. This is why executive succession is such a critical topic. In the family-owned firm, the question of executive succession is especially sensitive, because it concerns the continued role of the family in the business founded by an ancestor. Quite a few larger family firms have nonfamily executives, of course, with the family maintaining its voice as entrepreneur shareholders and, often but not always, occupying positions on the board of directors. Even in these cases, however, executive succession is a family affair – the candidate has to suit the family and reflect its values. The process of executive succession also raises a set of generic governance questions, irrespective of whether the firm is privately held or publicly listed: first, if the previous CEO is merely moving up to the chairmanship, is the succession really a succession? And, second, did the nomination committee apply a fair and open process, or was the decision precooked to reflect the special interests of some shareholders (or directors) over others? These questions go to the heart of determining who really has the power to direct the firm, and, if the answers prove unsatisfactory to some shareholders or board members, can lead to a reconsideration of the basic tenets of how the firm is governed.[19]

Change in risk profile

To many observers, corporate governance is primarily about rules and procedures: compliance, Sarbanes-Oxley, and so forth. This narrow view of the means of corporate governance obscures a broader view of the ends of corporate governance.[20] Why are the rules and procedures put in place to begin with? If we accept that corporate governance is in place to ensure the continued existence of the firm, then the procedures take on real meaning. As the businesses of the firm grow and change, the corporate governance procedures also need to evolve. As we have seen, new management is often associated with a change in strategy, by the design of shareholders or by the willpower of the executive. A new strategy, in turn, exposes the firm to new risks, and this is why executive succession should be followed up by a periodic review of measurement and control procedures. Consider the example of the American bank, CIT. CIT was (and is once again today) a significant lender to small and medium-sized enterprises, but starting in 2004, when Merrill Lynch investment banker Jeffrey Peek joined the bank as the new CEO, the bank embarked on a sustained expansion drive that resulted in significant exposure to high risk lending groups that the existing management reporting system could not accurately assess. As a direct consequence of the management change and the failure of the governance system in place, the global financial crisis hit CIT much harder than it would have otherwise, and the firm eventually had to be restructured with the help of the United States federal government.[21]

Because a new chief executive can take the firm in entirely new directions, executive succession is also about assessing risk to the firm. Particularly those executives that we classify as adopters will put existing control systems to a severe test. Each business is subject to its own specific type of risk, so there cannot be a one-size-fits-all solution to measuring and controlling for risk. We find that shareholders and boards of directors are often surprised at how quickly new executives and their teams can build up sizeable new risks, without adequate control in place. Shareholders and boards need to bear in mind the following causal relationships: a change in management can lead to a change in strategy which in turn may imply an increase in risk.

Point to watch: adapting governance to the new executive

Only very rarely do boards of directors or shareholders (when they are tasked with the appointment) consider the corporate governance implications of appointing a new executive. In light of the power transferred to the CEO, particularly in the United States where the CEO typically also takes on the role of chair of the board, this is hard to understand. By not considering the corporate governance implications of the appointment, decision-makers give the new CEO an opportunity to shape systems and controls to his/her liking. The board of directors, in particular, can be significantly weakened as a result. The point is not to shackle the new executive unnecessarily, but rather that decision-makers need to be fully aware of the implications of their choice – for strategy, for ownership, and for governance.

Change in the dominant coalition

The final and perhaps most significant governance impact of a change in management has to do with the balance of power in the firm. As we have seen in the case of TUI described in Chapter 1, over time, a new chief executive can work to entrench him or herself, forging alliances with certain shareholders against other shareholders and packing the board of directors with supporters.[22] Although this kind of behavior is more often observed in publicly listed firms with a preponderance of silent shareholders (traders and sleepers), it also happens in privately held firms, particularly larger, more mature family-owned firms in which there are multiple branches. In these kinds of privately held firms, like in publicly listed firms dominated by silent shareholders, there can be a power vacuum that allows a forceful executive to take control.

Yielding significant power over decision-making in the firm to the chief executive is not necessarily a bad thing; particularly in turnaround situations, an all-powerful CEO can be very effective. However, too much power in the hands of the executive becomes problematic when it is put in the service of the interests of a few, to the detriment of the long-term health of the firm, or when it blocks necessary changes as described in Chapter 6. This is why the executive succession process also must take into account the current and likely future balance of power in the firm.

Change in the identity of management – conclusion

The most important thing to keep in mind about a change in the identity of management is that it always has broader implications: for strategy, for ownership, and for governance. Executive succession is never merely about choosing a person for a job. On the contrary, if not handled with all the necessary circumspection, executive succession can fundamentally alter the long-term prospects of the firm.

Concluding remarks

We have presented two frameworks for describing the identity of shareholders and managers, respectively. Although they differ in terms of how are they defined, both of these frameworks revolve around the same core concepts: values and methods. Essentially, therefore, the analysis of the effect of a change in the identity of ownership or management on strategy and governance can be focused on a review of how the values and methods of ownership or management have shifted with new shareholders and new managers. If, contrary to agency theory, shareholders are not all alike and managers are not all alike, then understanding different values and different methods provides a more accurate perspective on how shareholders and managers interact to shape strategy and governance.

Shareholders assure confidence in the firm; managers assure competence in the execution of the firm's strategy. If the identity of shareholders or the identity of managers changes, both confidence in the future of the firm and competence in the execution of the firm's strategy will be affected. How these changes in the identity of shareholders and managers play out in practice also depends to no small degree on the context. In Part I, we took form of ownership and organization for granted, but because form also influences the behaviors of economic actors, we need to explain how changes in legal and organizational form constrain or enable shareholders and managers and, ultimately, affect strategy and governance.

Background reading – Part I

Carlock, R. S. and Ward, J. L. *Strategic Planning for the Family Business*. London: Palgrave Macmillan, 2001.

Cohan, W. D. *The Last Tycoons: The Secret History of Lazard Frères & Co.*, New York: Doubleday, 2007.

Finkelstein, S., Hambrick, D. A., and Canella, Jr., A. A. *Strategic Leadership: Theory and Research on Executives, Top Management Teams, and Boards*, New York: Oxford University Press, 2009.

Fisher, Philip A. *Common Stocks and Uncommon Profits*, New York: Harper & Bros, 1958.

Graham, B. and Dodd, D. *Security Analysis* (sixth edn.), New York: McGraw-Hill Professional, 2008.

Keynes, J. M. *General Theory of Employment, Interest, and Money*, London: Palgrave Macmillan, 1936.

Malkiel, B. G. *A Random Walk Down Wall Street: The Time-tested Strategy for Successful Investing*, New York: W.W. Norton, 1973.

Vancil, R. M. *Passing the Baton: Managing the Process of CEO Succession*, Cambridge, MA: Harvard Business School Press, 1987.

Zaleznik, A. and Kets de Vries, M. F. R. *Power and the Corporate Mind*, Boston: Houghton Mifflin, 1975.

Changes in the form of ownership and organization

In Part I, we explained how the identity of shareholders and managers affects the choice of strategy. We noted that shareholders and managers differ among themselves according to their values and methods. This means that the balance of power between shareholders and managers is more complex than described by agency theory. Rather than a simple opposition between the interests of shareholders and managers, there are in fact a variety of different shareholder and manager interests to consider in thinking through how the identity of shareholders and managers affects strategy. Our approach takes these differences into account and provides a clear framework for analyzing the variety of identities observed in business practice.

And yet, this is only a part of the story. There are many different constellations of the balance of power, and these do not depend solely on the identity of the shareholders and the managers. The context plays a critical role, determining to what extent different shareholders and different managers are *substitutable* without serious consequences to the firm. For example, a historical majority shareholder in a family firm cannot be replaced without engendering a profound change in the culture of the firm. Analogously, in a firm that is built around a highly centralized hierarchy, the executive cannot be replaced without serious repercussions for the firm. A priori, one cannot determine if the influence of a shareholder or a manager that is very difficult to replace is positive or negative, in performance terms. What can be said with certainty, however, is that the harder it is, *from a structural point of view*, to replace a shareholder or a manager, the greater the weight of that shareholder or manager in the balance of power that defines the governance of the firm.

In order to deepen our understanding of the relationship between changes in ownership and management and changes in strategy, we must therefore examine the forms of ownership and of organization. Our argument revolves around the notion of how substitutable a shareholder or a manager is: the more easily a shareholder or a manager is replaced, the less influence that actor will have on choosing the strategy of the firm. In practice, the ease with which shareholders and managers can be replaced depends to a large extent on the ownership structure (for the shareholder) and the organization structure (for the manager). This means that a change of ownership structure such as an IPO or a change of organization structure such as a decentralization of decision-making authority can change the balance of power among and between shareholders and managers, with consequences, ultimately, for the choice of the strategy of the firm.

In Chapter 4, we show how the internal hierarchical form of the firm (centralized or decentralized) gives more or less power to the executive and hence affects the ease with which the executive is substitutable. For example, if the hierarchy is increasingly centralized, the executive controls more and more of the systems of information and decision-making and will henceforth be more difficult to replace. By contrast, if decision-making is decentralized, it will be easier to replace the executive without risking consequences for the entire system. In other words, a change of organizational form is not governance neutral: it can increase the power of the executive and make him/her harder to replace or it can decrease the power of the executive and make him/her easier to replace. In order to anticipate changes in governance and strategy, it is also necessary to consider the evolution of organization form.

First, however, we turn our attention in Chapter 3 to ownership form. The argument is analogous, focusing on the ease with which shareholders are substitutable. Some ownership structures give more weight to shareholders than others because, under these structures, shareholders are less easily substitutable. Thus, if ownership is highly concentrated or if voting rights are in few hands, shareholders are not easily substitutable (i.e., in a firm dominated by a founder, a family, or a state, etc.). On the contrary, if the shareholding of a firm is publicly traded and widely dispersed, current shareholders have little capacity for individual action and are easily substitutable with other shareholders. Therefore, a change in ownership form will have a significant impact on to what extent and how shareholders can influence the firm. Contrary to received wisdom, going public and its opposite, going private, are not simply questions of financing. Decisions about ownership form have inevitable consequences for the balance of power among and between shareholders and managers and, *a fortiori*, on strategic choices.

THREE

Change in legal structure

In terms of number, firms owned by individuals and families constitute the vast majority of business enterprises around the world, typically over 90 percent in any country.[1] Where an equity market exists, many, but by no means all, of the larger firms are publicly listed. The principal structural difference between publicly listed firms and privately owned firms (as well as cooperatives and state-owned firms) is that in publicly listed firms shareholders are *substitutable*, whereas in the other forms, shareholders are not, or to a much lesser degree. Indeed, the existence of equity markets is based upon the substitutability of shareholders. If shareholders are not substitutable as in the case of family firms or partnerships, for example, the firm and its strategy are closely associated with *characteristic* shareholders: the family or the partners. The interests of the family, or the partners, give the firm its character, and strategy is chosen accordingly. Taking a firm public renders shareholders substitutable and anonymous, and this has important consequences for shareholders' involvement in strategy and strategy itself. Conversely, taking a firm private puts its strategy and its fortunes in the hands of characteristic shareholders. By examining the opposite extremes – going public and going private – we can see how fundamental changes in ownership form are linked to changes in strategy.[2]

For illustrative purposes, we start by describing the evolution of US investment banking, an industry in which all of the main players went through the transition from characteristic shareholders (the partners) to substitutable shareholders over the same twenty-year period.

US investment banking: change of ownership form, change of strategy

Prior to 1971, the US investment banking industry was dominated by six partnerships – in these firms, only partners who had had a successful career at the firm could be owners. Starting in 1971 with the initial public offering (IPO) of Merrill Lynch and culminating in 1999 with the going public of Goldman Sachs, all six of these firms changed ownership form (in between the IPOs of Merrill and Goldman, there were the IPOs of Salomon Bothers in 1981; of Bear Stearns in 1985; of Morgan Stanley in 1986; and of Lehman Brothers in 1994). Over the years following their going public, all six of these venerable institutions reorganized around distinct profit centers and took on considerably more risk. The tendency to privilege riskier trading and leveraged transactions for the bank's own account over the less spectacular, but steadier fee income from advisory services was further exacerbated as the identity of ownership shifted from partner majority to partner minority. Some observers have gone so far as to draw a direct line between the change in ownership form from partnership to publicly quoted company and the ultimate failure (or near failure) due to excessive risk taking of the five remaining firms in 2008[3]: the bankruptcy of Lehman Brothers, the takeovers of Bear Stearns and Merrill Lynch, and the revocation of investment banking status for Morgan Stanley and Goldman Sachs.[4]

Given that the IPOs of these institutions happened twenty and more years ago and that the environment for investment banking has changed considerably in the intervening time period, the failures of these investment banks cannot be traced solely to the change of ownership form. The investment banks took on outside capital because they could (the New York Stock Exchange prohibited investment banks from going public until 1970) and because they needed it to deal with increasing competition and increasing capital requirements in their traditional businesses (advice on transactions, issuing of securities, and trading for clients). The successive internet and mortgage lending bubbles also played a role in changing the risk cultures of these firms from the staid environment of the 1960s and 1970s to the casino atmosphere of the 2000s.[5]

However, it cannot be denied that all six changed strategic course dramatically in the years following their going public. Was it simply a matter of taking more risk when "playing with other people's money"?[6] This explanation is too simple – in all of these firms, managing partners retained substantial shareholdings and were therefore making bets not only with other people's money but also with their own. And yet, bringing in substitutable shareholders with no ownership commitment to any particular bank and external values changed the game for the investment banks and their managers. Whereas before going public, strategic decisions were made in light of relatively homogenous ownership interests (determined by internal values akin to those of Pictet described in Chapter 1) and the managing partners were also the sole shareholders, the years after going public brought an increasing diversity of interests into the picture, including traders who expected higher and higher returns on equity from the investment banks. Post-IPO, the position of the managing partner was multifaceted – now the managing partner was a substitutable shareholder and an employee who was paid very well out of earnings that also belonged, in part, to others. Moreover, the managing partner had only limited liability for the claims on the firm.[7] Not surprisingly, then, many managing partners ceased to act as characteristic shareholders.

Our argument is not that publicly listed firms always take on more risk than privately held firms.[8] Clearly, some privately held firms such as hedge funds are designed to take on very large amounts of risk, with the partners standing to lose everything in the event that the funds' bets do not pay off (especially if they are also personally invested). Rather, the case of the US investment banks illustrates the need to adopt a dynamic perspective on the relationship between ownership change and strategy change. The different, external values associated with the shareholders of a public corporation coupled with the change from partnership to limited liability help explain why the great US investment banks *all* eventually changed their strategic emphasis from the safety of servicing client needs to the riskiness of proprietary dealing. Once they were publicly listed firms with substitutable shareholders, their strategic choices followed a different logic from that espoused by characteristic shareholders.[9]

I. General considerations in going public

Initial public offerings represent a significant economic activity. In 2010, only two years after the deepest financial crisis since the Great Depression, the number of deals (1,468) and the total volume ($281 billion) was almost back to the highs of 2007, and the following year promised to break all the old records.[10] Previously concentrated in the US and Europe, today the market for IPOs is truly global, with some of the largest new issues coming out of China, India, and Brazil (the $19.1 billion raised by the Industrial and Commercial Bank of China in 2006 still stands as the single largest IPO). With so much money at stake, the business of going public attracts a lot of players, principally auditors, lawyers, and investment banks. In the eyes of these advisors, an IPO is not a so much a strategic, but first and foremost a legal cum financial transaction. From the point of view of this book, what is remarkable is the almost complete absence of strategy advisors in the IPO process. In other words, ownership and strategy are seen as independent.[11]

Point to watch: conflicting interests in an IPO

Decision-makers considering an IPO are usually well aware of the fact that auditors, lawyers, and investment banks have a strong interest in making a deal. These advisors all make far more money if the offering goes through than if it is merely evaluated as an option and are therefore very unlikely to recommend against going public (although they may recommend delaying if markets are weak). What decision-makers are less likely to think through is that existing shareholders as well as managers also have conflicting interests and that these conflicts may become exacerbated with the IPO. Thus, despite protestations to the contrary ex ante, some shareholders will not be able to withstand the temptation of selling out quickly, while some managers will take advantage of the dilution of power of the characteristic shareholders to push for more growth and more responsibility for themselves. An IPO changes the game for everyone involved.

To ensure transparency and gain access to capital (and currency) under the most favorable conditions, decision-makers in firms considering going public call on the help of outside experts. Months of meetings are spent with lawyers to work out shareholders' agreements that tie key people to the firm and to limit the power of outside shareholders; even more time goes into due diligence on accounts and fair evaluation. As a result, the package that finally comes to the market appears very well polished, a product that can be bought and enjoyed (or resold) without any surprises. Once the legal/financial transaction is completed, the firm can go back to doing business as usual; aside from the new inconveniences of quarterly reporting, independent directors, and investor relations, decision-makers in the firm are apparently free to pursue the strategy of their choice.

It would seem that the original characteristic shareholders do not anticipate much influence from the substitutable shareholders that come with a public listing. In theory, substitutable shareholders are unlikely to exercise their voice and will therefore allow decision-makers a great deal of discretion. And yet, somehow, the "markets" appear to exercise considerable influence over a firm that goes public. Going public involves opening up the firm to outside scrutiny and yielding some measure of power over the future of the firm to the markets. Why do firms volunteer to be subjected to outside influence?

Two classic reasons given for an IPO are capital for growth and liquidity for the shares. In the words of Marc Rich, the founding father of Glencore, the largest IPO in 2011, "I basically see two reasons for going public ... it is a way of funding your business and to finance growth. Plus, you have more liquid shares. It is easier to leave the company and redeem your shares."[12] Additionally, a listing on public markets permits assessment of the value of the firm and may enhance the reputation of a firm. The reasons generally given are summarized in Table 3.1.

It is important to differentiate the reasons for going public. The first, access to capital, is fundamentally different from the others in terms of the consequences for governance and strategy. Going public to gain access to capital does not put the firm under the sway of the capital markets – capital is raised according to objective, internal criteria of growth, and the sole role of substitutable shareholders is to provide funds. Going public to ensure liquidity, to assess the value of the firm, and to enhance the reputation of the firm, on the other hand, does make the firm strongly susceptible to the influence of the

TABLE 3.1 *Reasons for going public: reference points and values*

Reason for IPO	Reference point	Value
Access to capital	Internal growth targets	Internal
Liquidity of the share	Assessment of shareholders	External
Evaluation of the share	Assessment of shareholders	External
Reputation of the firm	Assessment of shareholders	External

capital markets. Liquidity, evaluation, and reputation are all external reference points that imply continuous maintenance long after the IPO is completed. The markets' verdict on liquidity, evaluation, and reputation is subject to change repeatedly, and the firm will need to take this verdict into account each time it makes strategic choices. In other words, in going public and exchanging characteristic shareholders for substitutable shareholders, the reasons for going public play an important role in explaining to what extent the capital markets can influence the strategy of the firm.

Point to watch: strategy advice and the IPO

What kind of strategy advice should a firm solicit prior to a planned IPO? The most relevant advice would center on comparing the firm to other firms in its industry that are public or have gone public. By looking at the strategies these firms are following, decision-makers considering an IPO can get a feeling for the expectations that new shareholders are likely to have and the ambitions that managers may harbor. Since going public is typically associated with growth, the critical question for decision-makers to gauge is how going public will influence the growth trajectory. Depending on shareholder expectations and manager ambitions, the growth trajectory may turn out much steeper, and therefore much riskier, than originally intended and that is what a strategic review of the industry can help decision-makers to think about before going public.

The reasons behind going public explain why the markets can exercise pressure on the firm, even if individual shareholders are substitutable and of little weight. The influence of the markets can be seen in how the strategy of a firm changes with the IPO: either prior to the IPO to please the markets, or after the IPO under the pressure of the markets.

Strategy changes prior to the IPO

Consider the example of India-based SKS Microfinance, the first Asian microfinance provider to go public (in 2010). Over the three and a half years from March 2006 to September 2009, SKS recorded a cumulative annual growth rate of around 250 percent. Meanwhile, its profit margins also rose dramatically, with return on equity increasing from 5.1 percent in FY2007 to 18.3 percent in FY2009. These rates of growth were unprecedented in the field of microfinance and made the company a very attractive IPO, especially to return-oriented investors who would not otherwise have considered entering the social responsibility sphere. How had these exceptional rates of growth been achieved? As early as 2003, in anticipation of raising outside funding (first from banks and eventually through the IPO), the company had begun to introduce a variety of scaling techniques borrowed from commercial banking – broad-based market outreach, standardized loan products, and tough collection processes, all supported by significant investment in information technology. By the time of the IPO in 2009, SKS no longer looked like a typical microfinance institution – the characteristic social bottom line mattered less than standard metrics of financial success in the lending business.[13] Given this pre-IPO history, it should have come as no surprise to shareholders that an economic slowdown would get SKS embroiled in controversy; and yet, many shareholders, and especially those with a focus on social responsibility (like Small Industries Development Bank of India or Catamaran Management Services), had to be horrified when, in 2010, the press linked the suicides of over a dozen farmers with the tough follow-up and coercive recovery processes employed by SKS. These shareholders had subscribed to the IPO without taking into proper consideration how much the strategy of SKS had changed in the years *leading up* to the IPO.[14]

In the case of Glencore, the relationship between strategy change and ownership change can be observed over an even longer period of time. Glencore started back in the 1970s as an oil trader, a go-between that did not operate any wells or refineries but stood between producers, shippers, and refiners. Over time, in order to be assured of long-term contracts and distribution rights the company started to invest in upstream production. This approach was subsequently applied to numerous other commodities, including copper and aluminum, to the point where today, Glencore has become an owner of commodities assets around the world that *also* trades. Where the lack of transparency that goes with being privately owned may have been an advantage for the trading company that Glencore used to be, it is no longer necessary for the asset owner that the company has become. For an asset owner like Glencore, access to fresh capital from the public is essential to further growth, and it is to be expected that going public will only reinforce the strategic shift from trading to asset ownership that has been under way for a long time. We do not wish to imply that the strategy of Glencore changed because of the plans for an IPO; however, considering the 2002 sale of Glencore's coal business to Xstrata in advance of *its* 2002 IPO, it seems reasonable to assume that the shareholders of the company have recognized for some time that the strategy of pursuing asset ownership would eventually require an IPO.[15]

If, as these examples show, strategy can change before a firm goes public, in part to make the firm more attractive to shareholders (i.e., SKS) or more easily understood by shareholders (i.e., Glencore), then considering a change of ownership form without thinking about the potential for strategy change can lead to serious misjudgments: the original shareholders may not realize how far away the prospect of an IPO can take the firm from its original strategy and business culture; new shareholders, on the other hand, may not be getting what they think they have signed up for. Both the original ownership group and new shareholders are well advised to carefully review the firm's strategy in the years leading up to an IPO.

Strategy changes after the IPO

In some cases, strategy changes before the actual IPO, in others the effect of the change in ownership only makes itself felt post-IPO. Interestingly, a change of strategy in the time period immediately following an IPO typically does not stem from any attempts of new shareholders to *directly* influence the course of the firm. In the early years, new shareholders are usually too small or too unfamiliar with the firm to effectively make their voices heard. Instead, it is the need to present shareholders with a compelling story and the numbers to support it that can lead decision-makers (often still the original ownership group) to alter the strategic course of the firm.

KPMG Consulting went public in February, 2001. At the time, the $2 billion IPO was the second largest in NASDAQ history. Going public was supposed to free the business from the constraints of operating under KPMG and give it the capital to pursue a strategy of global expansion. Having paid back most of the funds raised to the firm's original shareholders (the partners of KPMG), in the eighteen months following the IPO, KPMG Consulting used debt financing to acquire KPMG's consulting practices in Japan, Korea, New Zealand, Australia, China, Brazil, Germany, Austria, and Switzerland, as well as twenty-three consulting units from Arthur Andersen. Instead of building on these practices' strong local business ties and differentiated value propositions, KPMG Consulting (renamed Bearing Point at the end of 2002) aggressively pushed for IT service business around the world. This was what worked in the United States, and the new firm's management was determined to win with a one-size-fits-all approach. As it turned out, KPMG Consulting did not have the systems in place to manage and accurately report on such a global strategy, and the firm quickly ran into trouble.[16] After a series of resignations at the top and accounting irregularities throughout the firm, KPMG Consulting eventually filed for bankruptcy protection in 2009. In this case, the firm did do what it said it was going to do at the time of the IPO, but global expansion in IT services meant that it needed to fundamentally change the strategies of the local consulting practices. In other words, in order to deliver on the promise of the IPO, KPMG Consulting had to try to transform its new subsidiaries in a very short time. Given how tight resources were and in view of the difficulty of bringing about change in professional service organizations, KMPG Consulting's failure is not surprising; the IPO and the public markets' pressure for results contributed to accelerating the firm's downfall.

The case of a Russian tire manufacturer (Amtel) that engaged in a series of acquisitions and expanded into retail (of tires) following its 2005 IPO, illustrates a different twist on the need to present shareholders with a compelling story and the numbers to support it. In order to mask falling numbers in the manufacturing business, the original shareholder of the firm (who still held a majority of the shares) pushed it into a post-IPO strategy of growth by acquisition (Vredestein) and diversification that had not been part of the original prospectus. He hoped that the numbers (and the complexity) created by the acquisitions would satisfy the new shareholders' expectations for growth and help tide the firm over until the manufacturing business became profitable again. As events transpired, Amtel bit off more than it could handle and was forced into bankruptcy only four years after the IPO.[17] Would the firm have been able to follow the same reckless course if the company had not been listed? Perhaps a local bank would have loaned the money for expansion, but a local bank would not have been as easily satisfied that things were going well as foreign shareholders (such as Templeton Asset Management, Citicorp International Finance Corp., and Temasek from Singapore) who wanted to get a piece of the action in Russia (2005 was the biggest year for IPOs in Russia) and took the numbers at face value. Again, an IPO can be the first step in changing a firm's strategy.

Why does strategy (often) change with an IPO?

In the preceding pages, we described how strategy can change with an IPO, in some cases in the years leading up to the change of ownership, in others in the years immediately following the change. Of course, an IPO also has long-term effects on strategy, and these effects may not be felt for a number of years (as described in the case of the six US investment banks at the start of the chapter). Going public creates a new incentive context for both shareholders and managers, including those shareholders and managers who were with the company before the IPO. With the addition of outside shareholders and the change of status of former characteristic shareholders to employees, decision-makers are faced with the problem of finding a way to create unity out of dissimilar (and sometimes conflicting) interests. Consequently, strategy becomes a variable to manipulate in the search of a common denominator among different interest groups (with different values).

In some cases, the strategy changes that go with an IPO are voluntary, in the sense that decision-makers in the firm utilize the IPO and the introduction of substitutable shareholders to make desired changes in the strategy. In other cases, the strategy changes that go with an IPO occur under pressure, in response to market demands. In general, we can say that the more important the considerations of liquidity, evaluation, and reputation in prompting the IPO, the more likely a significant strategic change with the IPO. The long-term evidence on companies that have gone public shows that their strategies change, not only in response to competitive shifts, but also in order to provide a coherent incentive context for a changing coalition of shareholders and managers.[18] Indeed, the strategic changes described earlier, both pre-IPO as in the cases of SKS and Glencore, or post-IPO as in the cases of KPMG Consulting and Amtel, and even longer-term strategic shifts like those of the leading US investment banks can be understood in light of the perceived need to reconcile the different and varying interests of shareholders and managers.

Point to watch: multiple shareholders in an IPO

Where there are only a few characteristic shareholders, such as in the case of an internet startup with a small team of founders or a family business still run by the founder and the nuclear family, an IPO has only a few people to satisfy. The situation becomes much more complex if the firm considering an IPO has a sizable number of shareholders (in the case of a larger partnership) or even a multitude of shareholders (in the case of a cooperative). In larger partnerships and, especially, in cooperatives, an IPO will significantly dilute the influence of the average characteristic shareholder. In general, the average characteristic shareholder, that is the shareholder who is not large enough to maintain his/her influence after an IPO, suffers from poorer business conditions after going public, as the firm moves away from its original mission of serving all characteristic shareholders equally. The initial windfall of turning shares or membership into cash is small compensation.

Attempts to prevent a post-IPO change of strategy

Although thinking about the relationship between ownership change and strategy change is not high on the agenda of most IPO decision-makers and advisors, several firms have made significant efforts to make sure that their IPO does not lead to a strategic change that runs counter to the interests of the original owners. Most famously, Berkshire Hathaway and, following in Warren Buffett's footsteps, Google, have sought to structure the shareholders' agreement in such a way that the influence of outside shareholders is kept at bay. The most common way of doing this is the dual share structure in which different classes of shares have different voting rights. At Google's IPO, for example, Class B shares that have ten voting rights were restricted to insiders (founders, directors, management); new shareholders only had access to Class A shares with one voting right. This made it possible for the two founders, Larry Page and Sergey Brin, together with Eric Schmidt, the CEO they had handpicked, to control 60 percent of the voting power with only 38 percent of the total shares outstanding following the IPO in 2004.[19]

Google, unlike most firms going public (but similar to more recent high tech IPO stars like Facebook and Zynga, which followed Google in imposing two classes of shares), was in a position to dictate the terms of its IPO, without suffering any measurable decline in interest from shareholders. Liquidity, evaluation, and reputation did not seem to matter to Google when it went public, and, even, today, eight years later, do not seem to concern the firm's decision-makers very much. In a sense, Google is big enough and strong enough to disregard the markets, a kind of Gulliver in a world in which most listed firms are heavily influenced by financial markets in their choices of governance and strategy (see Chapter 1). And yet, one wonders if control of voting rights will be enough, in the long term, for Google to avoid the markets' influence on strategy. The day may yet come, when the company fails to perform as expected, the major shareholders' interests start to diverge, or individual managers seeking to maximize personal gain as shareholder/employees, start to take parts of the company in new directions that, collectively, constitute a major shift in strategy that is at least in part attributable to the IPO and the attendant change in the incentive context. Already in the eight years since the IPO, the company has seen a plethora of strategic initiatives, not all of which appear justified from a characteristic shareholder's point of view.

More generally, the founders' maintaining a controlling interest after going public has not in and of itself prevented companies from changing strategy to accommodate "the markets." Although still controlled by the founding family, French tire giant Michelin famously attributed the decision to lay off workers after announcing record profits in 1999 to pressure from foreign and especially American pension funds.[20] Over time, the interests of controlling shareholders tend to diverge and new managers with new values enter the scene; these processes make the firm more vulnerable to outside influences, especially if results do not hold up. An IPO breaks the unity of interest that characterizes family-owned firms and firms based on shared interests like partnerships and cooperatives that have strong internal values.

> **Point to watch: maintaining influence without a majority**
>
> Some family firms have been able to maintain influence over the long-term evolution of the firm their ancestors founded even after going public. In these cases, the family has not limited its involvement to restrictive shareholder agreements that give the family greater voting rights, but stayed active in the business, in executive and/or board roles. Just as importantly in these cases, the family has been able to imprint its business culture on the firm so that even where the family is not directly involved in decision-making, their principles are explicitly referred to. (For an example of this form of positive family influence, see the extensive description in Chapter 5 of how the Beaudoin family continues to provide guidance for the Canadian transportation giant Bombardier, many decades after going public.)

Firms can try to reduce the scope of outside influence by crafting purposeful shareholder agreements and can also try to attract the kind of shareholders they want. Firms should carefully consider the likely constraints on strategy following changes in ownership form, before they take the plunge. The important thing to remember is that an IPO's effect on strategy cannot be reduced to a question of control. Going public brings in new players with different values (implying different levels of commitment to the firm) and so fundamentally changes the incentives of shareholders and managers. This means that one can guard against, but can never entirely eliminate the possibility that going public leads to strategy change. Decision-makers should take a dynamic view of ownership, management, and strategy. Going public is only the first step in navigating the challenges of changes in ownership form.

II. General considerations in going private

One of the most striking findings in our review of the literature of changing ownership form concerns the diametrically opposed approaches adopted in considering going public and going private: whereas going public is primarily thought of in legal and financial terms, going private is thought of as a choice for change in how decisions are made.[21] Going public is seen as a transaction; going private is seen as a fundamental shift in the governance of the firm. Given what we have described about the strategic implications of going public, this opposition does not appear justified, and we can only speculate on its origins and the reasons for its persistence. Going private is less complex, from a legal and a financial point of view; it involves a smaller number of stakeholders and, perhaps crucially, does not attract special attention from regulators. Furthermore, unlike in the case of going public, where substantial fees can be earned right away and do not depend on the strategy of the firm, the bulk of the benefits of going private take longer to accrue and are necessarily the result of strategic and organizational changes. Whatever the ultimate reasons for the opposition, there can be no doubt that going public and going private, although two sides of the same coin, represent two entirely different markets, with different players and different issues.

Strategic reasons for going private

What are the reasons for firms to (delist and) go private? Irrespective of the type of buyer – another business firm or a private equity investor (group) – inefficiencies in public equity markets play an important role in going private.[22] These inefficiencies come under two headings: pricing and decision-making. The pricing argument for going private holds that, in some cases, public equity markets consistently undervalue a particular firm, and taking that firm private represents a good buy – getting assets for less than they are really worth. A firm can be undervalued for any number of reasons: too small to get the attention of analysts, not transparent enough to allow accurate valuation, not managed in such a way as to release the full earnings power of the assets, too complicated a shareholding structure to permit strategic change, etc. The last two sources of undervaluation already hint at the decision-making argument for going private. In some publicly listed firms, poor management has become entrenched and cannot be unseated, because no individual shareholder or group of shareholders has the power necessary to force the board of directors to act; in others, important shareholders are at loggerheads, and critical decisions cannot be taken (see also Chapter 6). Differences of interests between management and shareholders and among shareholders that are inherent in public companies can be resolved by going private and putting the firm under the direction of a single point of view.[23]

It is worth stressing that the decision-making argument for going private is directly tied to strategy. Something needs to be done to get the firm back on track; at the very least the strategy needs to be reviewed and updated, but the diversity of views in the public company blocks the necessary action. In other words, in order to gain the freedom to change management and/or to change strategy, it may sometimes be essential to take the firm private. It is therefore not surprising that going private is almost invariably associated with such changes, and the existing literature, particularly on private equity, makes this abundantly clear. For business firms that go private again after having once gone public or privately owned business firms that take a public firm private as well as for private equity investors, fixing the strategy of the firm is at the top of an explicit agenda for change.

Different types of buyers, different outcomes

Depending on the buyer, we can differentiate two broad types of going private: by business firm or by private equity. The former type includes both business firms that go private again after having once gone public (i.e., Hilti, the Liechtenstein-based giant of construction technology that went public in 1986 and private again in 2003) or privately owned business firms that take a public firm private.[24] The latter includes going privates as well-known and large as Chrysler, AllianceBoots, or TXU and is represented by giant investor groups like Kohlberg Kravis Roberts or the Carlyle Group, as well as hundreds of smaller players. The essential difference between going private by business firm and going private by private equity is in the nature of the shareholder: whereas private equity typically sells a firm to an industrial buyer or brings it back to the public equity markets within a three-to-five year time frame and can therefore be classified as a characteristic shareholder with an external value (market valuation), private business firms, as characteristic shareholders with internal values, seek to put a lasting imprint on the firm taken private.[25] This difference of shareholder type has a direct effect on the kind of strategy changes implemented: turnaround and dressing up for sale by private equity, integration, and continuous improvement for private business firms.

Point to watch: advantages of private equity

Private equity with 100 percent ownership has the great advantage over many other forms of ownership that the question "strategy for whom?" does not need to be asked. From the closing of a private equity transaction, it is clear that everyone, from partners to managers to employees, is working for one and the same purpose. This may or may not be in the best long-term interests of the firm as a going concern, but it does have the great advantage of making objectives absolutely clear. The situation is much more complicated where private equity is only a partial owner in a business. In the case of shared ownership, private equity plays the role of activist, prodding management in a variety of ways (ideally including seats on the board and influence over the choice of managers) and persuading other shareholders to go along. Shared ownership puts the political skills of private equity to a very difficult test.

Changes to strategy prior to going private/after going private

Analogous to our analysis of going public, we can think about changes to strategy prior to going private and changes to strategy after going private. Since the whole point of going private is typically to enable changes that are not possible for the firm as a publicly listed entity, it is not surprising that changes prior to going private are typically limited to cosmetic adjustments that can facilitate the sale. The most frequent example of this kind of cosmetic adjustment is found in the sale of business units that have been weaned from the corporate structure in preparation for sale.

Where a diversity of interests blocks change in the publicly listed firm, however, any significant strategic shift has to wait for the new shareholder to take over. Changes to strategy after going private typically occur in two steps: (a) making the move that was prevented by the diversity of interests; and then (b) either integrating the firm into a larger whole (in the case of going private by a business firm) or preparing the firm for resale (in the case of going private by private equity). The first step after unblocking often involves a sale of unwanted assets and an optimization of the performance of the remaining business(es), with or without the previous management, depending on its willingness and ability to make the changes required by the new shareholders. The second step is context specific and may or may not involve further adjustment of the strategy.

Thinking about going private

Reporting requirements for publicly listed firms have increased dramatically in the last ten years; moreover, shareholders with external values have made large inroads into the decision-making independence of public firms, routinely demanding to be consulted on questions of strategic significance. Under these circumstances, many managers yearn for the relative simplicity of the private firm. Indeed, some observers have offered going private as a panacea for many of the ills affecting the publicly listed firm: over-investment in compliance, short-term focus, vulnerability to herd-like behavior, etc. But is going private really a panacea? Might it not be the wrong or too strong a medicine in many cases?

The key question to ask is whether going private is really a necessary prerequisite for changing the strategy and/or the management of a firm. As described in Chapter 1 and Chapter 6, activists who take smallish stakes and work behind the scenes to bring about change in cases of decision deadlock, can be very effective without having to pay the acquisition premium.[26] Of course, having a single interest around which to focus the firm can be extremely useful in certain well-defined contexts, particularly the management of turnarounds (with the attendant need to sell assets and optimize operations) or the buildup of scale economies (with the attendant need to focus the minds of managers and improve collaboration across boundaries). However, because going private can also isolate the firm from the pulse of public opinion and make it more difficult to keep up with fast-moving markets, it is imperative that plans for staying private (i.e., not private equity based) include alternative approaches for staying connected.

Point to watch: effects of size

Increased regulation, with the attendant requirements for investment in compliance and reporting, have significantly raised the cost of remaining publicly listed in the years since the collapse of Enron (2001). For firms in the financial services sector, the failures arising from the subprime crisis further tightened the noose. In some cases, the cost of keeping up with regulations represents such a high percentage of revenues that staying listed is simply not economically viable anymore. Instead of going private, most of these smaller firms have sought to be acquired by larger firms. As a perverse result of increased regulation, the number of firms still in the game has decreased and therefore so has competition. Of course, bigger firms also present greater challenges in compliance and reporting, so systemic risk has actually increased in a number of industries.

Change of ownership structure – conclusion

Going public is likely to be associated with changes in the strategy of the firm. Either before or, more commonly, after the IPO, the interplay of the different interests of shareholders and managers will lead to a redefinition of strategy. Such a redefinition of strategy may be explicit and immediately visible, as in the case of KPMG Consulting, or take shape in the minds of managers and take place over a period of years, as observed with the six US investment banks that gave up their historic partnership structures in order to go public.

Going private, like going public, needs to be seen in light of the diverse values of shareholders and managers. The decision to go private is usually tied to achieving a specific strategic objective, one that some shareholders and some managers do not share. In this sense, going private is a means for realigning the interests of shareholders and managers.

Transitioning from private to public means trading characteristic shareholders for substitutable shareholders (and vice versa). As we have shown in this chapter, opening the ownership structure to substitutable shareholders generally leads to fundamental changes in governance and strategy – *despite* the fact that substitutable shareholders, as individuals, have little power. Unless it can be assured that managers and key shareholders maintain internal values, the firm that goes public is likely to become increasingly market driven: for every market-dominating Gulliver like Google, there are dozens of firms for which going public implies subordinating strategy to the demands of the market.

Going public, and to a lesser extent, going private, are often reduced to a question of techniques applied by lawyers and investment bankers. The key question decision-makers considering going public/private should ask, in our view, revolves around shareholder substitutability. As summarized in Table 3.2 below, transitioning to an open ownership structure with easy shareholder substitutability (i.e., going public) always comes with the risk that the firm will reorient its strategy towards external values to reconcile the different interests of shareholders and managers. Transitioning to a closed ownership structure (i.e., going private), on the other hand, means entrusting the strategy of the firm to the specific designs of characteristic shareholders, market preparatory plans for shareholders with external values like private equity funds, or market neutral plans for shareholders with internal values like families and partnerships.

TABLE 3.2 *Consequences of a change of ownership form: shareholder values and shareholder substitutability*

		Shareholder substitutability	
		Easy (Open ownership structure)	Difficult (Closed ownership structure)
Values (shareholders)	External	- *Market driven*	- *Market preparatory*
	Internal	- *Market dominating*	- *Market neutral*

FOUR

Change in organizational structure

A change in ownership form requires the approval of shareholders and represents a major and rare event in the life of a business firm. A change in organizational structure, on the other hand, ostensibly has nothing to do with shareholders and occurs much more frequently. Should shareholders concern themselves with questions of internal organization? Reorganization stands for much more than the redrawing of organization charts. In fact, reorganization is one of the most far-reaching tools of change; it shifts the locus of power and affects how information is processed in the firm; as a result, reorganization almost always has significant long-term effects on the direction of the firm.[1] This is why we devote a chapter to the topic of reorganization in a book about firm ownership, management, and strategy.

Point to watch: the broader effects of reorganization

Looking at reorganization as a purely internal matter of concern only to management and employees unjustly ignores the broader effects that reorganization can have. Reorganization can be good for some shareholders and bad for others and good for some managers and bad for others. It affects the balance of power in the firm, strengthening or weakening different actors and changing how information is processed and communicated. And yet, reorganization is typically left to consultants to prepare and managers to decide – only very rarely does the board of directors, or share-holders, get involved. This is a risk that boards and shareholders should not take lightly.

I. Reorganization and corporate governance

Reorganization appears to be the one constant of life in organizations. From small firms reassigning responsibilities to better reflect changed market realities to large, multinational firms redesigning control systems to better meet changed requirements for information processing, reorganization happens all the time and everywhere. Used in so many different contexts, the term can take on a great variety of meanings. In this book, we focus on change of the reporting structure.[2] Change of the reporting structure revolves around change in relationships – who reports to whom for what – and reflects a revised point of view on what would make the firm perform better – an emphasis on greater individual responsibility (decentralization) versus an emphasis on greater shared responsibility (centralization). Typically, firms' reporting structures oscillate back and forth between greater individual responsibility and greater shared responsibility.[3]

Reorganization is closely tied to strategy change. In the classic case of structure following strategy, reorganization is supposed to enhance the implementation of a strategy change, making the organization more effective at doing what it is supposed to do and easier to monitor and guide in the right direction.[4] This is why strategy changes are typically accompanied by reorganizations and explains why people are worried when they are not. During the financial crisis of 2008, for example, it became apparent that many banks had decided to take on significantly more risk in their strategy, without making commensurate changes in their reporting structures and risk control systems. In the contrary case of strategy following structure, reorganization can prepare the firm for taking on a new strategy.

For example, restructuring around small entrepreneurial units can pave the way for rapid geographical expansion.[5]

Even when reorganization does not have an explicitly strategic objective, it can have consequences for strategy. For years, senior partners at Goldman Sachs were loath to emphasize individual contributions in measuring and rewarding performance: in the words of Managing director John Weinberg, this would lead to "plunging," i.e., individuals taking excessive risk on behalf of the firm for the chance of personal benefit.[6] Clearly, time has borne out the wisdom of that particular apprehension: one of the unintended consequences for investment banks of basing measurement and reward on individual performance has been a pronounced upsurge of risk exposure at the level of the firm.

Reorganization can also be a source of conflict and have an impact on the balance of power in the senior management team.[7] If the differences among custodians, technocrats, and adopters (or transformers) in the senior management team are pronounced, then any discussion about reorganization will exacerbate these. Custodians will not want to reorganize, technocrats will want to adapt to function or industry standards, and adopters will put the anticipated reaction of equity markets at the top of the agenda. Clearly, there will be winners and losers among the senior management team in the discussion and in the eventual reorganization that takes place (for example in terms of which function or business is rewarded), and this will have repercussions on the future direction of the firm.

More generally, reorganization towards centralization and greater shared responsibility reduces the ease of substituting of senior managers, while reorganization towards decentralization and greater individual responsibility makes it easier to substitute senior managers. This is because greater centralization gives the top management team more control over corporate-level information, making them harder to replace as a group. Decentralization, on the other hand, puts more responsibility at the individual level and divides the top management group, making it easier to remove individual managers on a case-by-case basis. The question of how reorganization influences the substitutability of senior managers should be of considerable interest to shareholders, as it directly affects the balance of power between shareholders and managers. The more easily substitutable the senior managers, the more temporary their engagements are likely to be, with strategy choices likely to be biased toward the short term.

If reorganization has an impact on strategy, risk, and management, then it is not governance neutral. In particular, changes in reporting relationships will have effects on the kind of information that is available to decision-makers.[8] Reorganization can shift the basis of how results are communicated, from larger units to smaller units of analysis and vice versa. Even if the information presented is ostensibly more precise in the micro, such as is the case for the individual performance of traders in investment banks, it may not be more accurate on a systemic basis, and may lead to a poorly integrated appreciation of the results of the firm. It is not only a question of how information is communicated, but also of how the kind of information that is used affects the incentives of people to work for themselves or for the good of the firm. If reorganization reinforces cooperation (whatever the mode of cooperation in the firm), the firm becomes easier to control; if, on the other hand, it leads to dissension and increased parochialism, the firm becomes harder to control, with the attendant governance concern of decision-makers not able to be sure of what is really going on in the deepest reaches of the organization.[9]

Quite apart from the impact on information and control, reorganization can make it easier or harder to value a firm and hence affect the ease of sale.[10] Generally, reorganization that breaks the firm into smaller, more clearly defined administrative units, such as business units, makes it easier to sell the individual components of the firm; reorganization that emphasizes greater shared responsibility and draws tighter links among units makes it less likely that the firm will be dismantled and sold off in pieces.[11] A change of control and performance measurement will, at a minimum, change the type and quality of information that is presented to shareholders. As we have seen, reorganization of this nature can also fundamentally affect the risk exposure of the firm. Whether reorganization is a good thing or a bad thing for shareholders ultimately depends on their values. What we can be certain about is that reorganization is not a matter of indifference to ownership.

II. Reorganization and the life cycle of the firm

As pointed out earlier, organization structures tend to oscillate back and forth between greater individual responsibility and greater shared responsibility. When the firm is young and relatively small, it is typically structured as a functional organization, the so-called U-Form. This organization is based on comprehensive oversight from the top and shared responsibility among the functions for the output of the firm. As the firm grows in size and complexity, to encompass multiple products (or services) and maybe also different geographic implantations, it is common to reorganize into an M-Form.[12] The M-Form is characterized by the creation of separate units for the different products (or services) under their own management teams and implies much greater individual responsibility. Over time, the M-Form also requires tinkering, perhaps to make the units even more independent (greater individual responsibility, increased decentralization) or to tie the separate units more closely together again (greater shared responsibility, increased centralization). Most larger, mature organizations have adopted some type of M-Form structure and evolve in a process of back and forth reorganization between greater individual responsibility and greater shared responsibility. Table 4.1 below presents reorganization in terms of its aims and implications and provides examples of changes to the organization structure.

TABLE 4.1   *Reorganization: aims and implications*

		Examples	General implications
Aim of reorganization	Greater individual responsibility	U-Form to M-Form HQ to NO's spin-off →	*Individual performance* *Decentralized information* *Higher manager substitutability*
	Greater shared responsibility	M-Form to U-Form NO to regions to HQ Integration (synergy) →	*Collective performance* *Centralized information* *Lower manager substitutability*

Reorganization – greater individual responsibility

Reorganization toward greater individual responsibility can take many forms: from a functional organization (U-Form) to a divisional organization (M-Form); from an international division at headquarters (HQ) to national organizations (NO) at the country level; or even a partial spinoff. Such reorganization may be supported by simultaneous changes in the control and performance measurement systems (i.e., information, indicators, and incentives focused on individual performance), but these changes can also came at a later date, to reinforce the move toward greater individual responsibility. Given that larger organizations typically oscillate back and forth between emphasizing shared and individual responsibility, changes in control and performance systems toward greater individual responsibility can also signal the end of a cycle toward greater shared responsibility. Once the M-Form is in place, often in the outward shape of a matrix organization, reorganization occurs in a more subtle manner: it is often more a question of what variables management emphasizes than a question of outward structural change.[13]

What to watch for in reorganization toward greater individual responsibility, from the points of view of strategy, governance, and ownership? Reorganization toward greater individual responsibility brings more clarity to decision-making in the firm. This is especially valuable in the context of rapid growth, precisely when firms like to increase individual responsibility. However, when coupled with rapid growth, greater individual responsibility also increases risks: the risk of inadequate due diligence in deals, the risk of insufficient attention to synergies across organizational boundaries, and the risk of overdependence on a few star managers.[14] In cases like these, there is a danger that critical information does not flow back to the center quickly enough and governance systems do not keep up. In other words, reorganization toward greater individual responsibility can also imply that the business gets ahead of control systems, making it harder for insiders and outsiders to evaluate the quality of a firm's financial performance.

In any case, shareholders therefore need to be particularly vigilant, when greater individual responsibility accompanies significant new growth initiatives. Recall from Chapter 1 that, in a publicly listed company, rapid growth can attract shareholders looking to make a quick killing, sometimes in coalition with a management team that has individual incentives to favor the short term. Whereas traders getting on for a short ride up do not really need to be concerned with how the growth strategy eventually pans out, entrepreneurs and sleepers who are committed to the firm cannot be sanguine about the increased risk and decreased reporting reliability that often comes with reorganizations aimed at greater individual responsibility. Analogously, in a privately held company, the early sparkle of rapid growth may seduce some shareholders to try to sell out early. Once the source of early growth dries up and concrete results have to be demonstrated, however, remaining shareholders will be left holding the bag. Ultimately, it is important for all shareholders to recognize that any move toward greater individual responsibility in the organization bears both opportunities and risks and may pit shareholders with different values against each other.

We have argued that decentralization tends to increase the substitutability of managers. What these managers actually do to deal with the prospect of increased substitutability depends on their values. Senior managers with external values (especially the managers that we have termed "adopters") pursue market-driven strategies, and this tendency is further exacerbated under conditions of easy management substitutability: knowing that they can be more easily replaced, these managers will turn to strategies that allow them to prove their worth to the market in a short time, such as major change initiatives or efforts to occupy new market space. Whether these work out or not, managers with external values will have prepared themselves to move on. Senior managers with internal values, by contrast, are likely to respond to decentralization by adhering even more closely to entrepreneur-driven strategies, so as not to fall out with the entrepreneur or key shareholder(s). This will help protect them from replacement, in times of easy management substitutability.

Reorganization – greater shared responsibility

Reorganization toward greater shared responsibility is often associated with periods of consolidation. Economy of scale, synergy, and headcount reduction are the watchwords, as management tries to squeeze more profit out of the existing customer base by enjoining disparate units to use fewer resources and cooperate more closely. The M-Form organization is a good candidate for this kind of reorganization, as is the multinational firm organized around independent national organizations. Again, the question is one of emphasis, particularly on control and performance measurement, and not necessarily on organization structure.[15] Thus, Nestlé's $5 billion and multiyear Globe project, for example, aimed at building a common infrastructure of information for the firm to better coordinate resource planning, purchasing, and distribution around the world: it was not accompanied by a change in the organization structure, but it nonetheless forced the national organizations to cooperate much more closely than they had in the past.[16]

What to watch for in reorganization toward greater shared responsibility, from the points of view of strategy, governance, and ownership? A focus on consolidation and greater shared responsibility can obscure new growth opportunities. The firm becomes fixated on internals and may therefore miss chances to expand into new areas. This can also become a governance concern, as decision-makers privilege information on the progress of consolidation and ignore signs of external threat.[17] Typically, the gains from consolidation programs supported by greater shared responsibility take several years to show up in the firm's results.

In the publicly listed firm, some shareholders (i.e., traders and activists) will not want to wait as long as it takes for the financial results to demonstrate the benefits of reorganization and will try to sell their shares, in some cases leading to price declines so steep that management will rethink the consolidation program. It is no accident that it was Nestlé, a firm that is relatively immune from the pressure of having to satisfy market expectations (see Chapter 1), who could embark on a project as long term and as ambitious as Globe. Various sources indicate that a similar project to improve the quality of shared information was rejected at a major Swiss bank, because executives were not willing to take a hit to short-term earnings.[18] For the privately held firm, shareholder patience may also be a problem; it depends on the values of the different shareholder groups and the balance of power among them. In general, reorganization toward greater shared responsibility signals that a period of consolidation is the offing: over time, consolidation is likely to strengthen the firm, but not all shareholders and not all managers will be willing to sit this period out.

Point to watch: paying for the cost of reorganization

The fact that the costs of reorganization begin to hit immediately, while the benefits of reorganization may, or may not, materialize over the medium term makes reorganization a potential source of conflict among and between managers and shareholders with different values. Senior managers who have a short time frame of engagement will typically try to delay reorganization so that it does not impact their performance figures (and bonuses). For this reason, the types of reorganization that involve large upfront investment (such as enterprise resource planning overhauls) are especially prone to being put off. Board members and shareholders focused on internal values need to bear this asymmetry in mind when evaluating the costs and benefits of reorganization.

If centralization tends to decrease the substitutability of managers, then this will also have an effect on strategy. Again, the nature of the effect will depend on the values of the senior managers. Managers with external values will take advantage of the increased difficulty of substitution associated with centralization to strengthen their power base and solidify their ties with the markets. In this case, one can expect strategic choices to be dominated by the interests of a coalition between managers and those actors in the financial markets who benefit most from a strategic focus on consolidation. By contrast, managers with internal values will try to benefit from an increased difficulty of substitution to pursue strategies that align with their own long-term interests. Here, one can expect strategies that further solidify managerial power and may run counter to the demands of the markets, eventually attracting activists bent on removing the managers. The consequences for strategy of a change in organizational form taking the values of senior managers into consideration are summarized in Table 4.2 below.

TABLE 4.2 *Consequences of a change of organizational form:*
manager values and manager substitutability

		Manager Substitutability	
		Easy (Decentralized org structure)	Difficult (Centralized org structure)
Values (Manager)	External	- *Market driven*	- *Manager/market coalition*
	Internal	- *Entrepreneur driven*	- *Manager driven*

Reorganization – conclusion

Like a modification of ownership form, reorganization is a structural change that has broader implications for strategy, ownership, and governance. Accompanying strategic change, reorganization can be a powerful basis for implementation; preceding strategic change, it can prepare the way for taking the firm in a new direction. Whether aimed at greater individual responsibility or at greater shared responsibility, reorganization is never merely a neutral tool, and shareholders need to pay careful attention to what it means for strategy and governance. Reorganization can presage growth or consolidation, with a concomitant increase or decrease in risk, and therefore it will not have the same effect on all shareholders. Reorganization also has an effect on the substitutability of senior managers, weakening or strengthening their position in the firm. The evidence shows that the less easily substitutable the management becomes, the more difficult it is for shareholders to shape strategy. In any case, a change in the structure of the organization will have an impact on how senior managers conceive of their position in the firm, making them more or less likely to pursue a given strategic direction.

PART II

Concluding remarks

In Part I, we argued that changes in the identity of shareholders or in the identity of managers affect confidence in the future of the firm and competence in the execution of the firm's strategy. In Part II, we have explained how changes in legal and organizational form constrain or enable shareholders and managers and, ultimately, affect strategy and governance. Building on the frameworks presented in Part I, we introduced a further core concept, the substitutability of shareholders and managers, as a means of understanding the mechanism by which changes in legal and organizational form shift the balance of power in the firm. Thus, how shareholders and managers act to shape strategy and governance depends not only on their values and methods, but also on how easy the legal and organizational form of the firm allows shareholders and managers, respectively, to be substituted. The more easily shareholders and/or managers are substituted, the weaker their commitment to a given strategy.

We now turn our attention to the question of how changes in strategy affect shareholders and managers. This may be seen as merely the other side of the coin, but, in reality, it has to be acknowledged that, just as changes in ownership and management can affect strategy, changes in strategy can lead to shifts in ownership, as shareholders who are not satisfied with the chosen strategy exit, and shifts in management, as managers who oppose the strategy leave the firm.

Background reading – Part II

Chandler, A. *Strategy and Structure: Chapters in the History of the American Industrial Enterprise*, Cambridge, MA: MIT Press, 1962.

Eccles, R. G. and Nohria, N. *Beyond the Hype: Rediscovering the Essence of Management*, Cambridge, MA: HBS Press, 1992.

Galbraith, J. R. *Designing Matrix Organizations That Actually Work: How IBM, Procter & Gamble, and Others Design for Success*, San Francisco: Jossey-Bass, 2009.

Greenberg, A. and Singer, M. *The Rise and Fall of Bear Stearns*, New York: Simon & Schuster, 2010.

Knee, J. A. *The Accidental Investment Banker*, New York: Random House, 2006.

Williamson, O. *Markets and Hierarchies*, New York: Free Press, 1975.

Changes in strategy

As presented in the first two parts of the book, changes in ownership and changes in management can, and frequently do, imply changes in strategy. What about the other way around – do changes in strategy lead to changes in ownership and in management, and if so, by what mechanisms and under what circumstances? The field of strategy is traditionally divided into two questions: corporate strategy – what businesses and markets a firm chooses to be in; and business strategy – what position a firm occupies and what resources a firm utilizes to compete in a given industry or market.[1] Whereas corporate strategy has been and continues to be a subject of debate among shareholders and finance specialists, with the attendant articulation of agency theoretical considerations about ownership and management, business strategy has been left to managers and economists, and its implications for ownership and corporate governance have remained largely unexplored.[2] We will show that changes in business strategy, by affecting risk, also raise significant governance questions that both managers and shareholders need to be aware of.

The effects of changes in both corporate strategy and business strategy are covered in Chapter 5. Changes in strategy are usually associated with rises and falls in the fortunes of a firm; in fact, success in the marketplace is the ultimate measure of the suitability of a strategy.[3] In the context of examining changes in strategy, it is therefore also of interest to examine when strategic change may be *blocked*: Chapter 6 looks at cases where no changes occur in ownership, management, and strategy – *despite failure* in the marketplace; Chapter 7 studies examples in which market *success reinforces* the existing constellation of ownership, management, and strategy.

FIVE

Corporate and business strategies

Significant changes in corporate or business strategy imply corresponding changes in capital needs, changes in management competence requirements, and changes in information processing structures. Therefore, such changes in strategy are always of interest to ownership, management, and corporate governance. In practice, the key step is to recognize what kind of changes in corporate and business strategy can take the firm into new territory and to adapt ownership, management, and corporate governance accordingly. As the case descriptions and the analysis in the following pages will show, significant changes in corporate or business strategy have the potential to undermine the long-run viability of the firm. Too often, the broader governance implications of changes in strategy are not recognized or are dealt with inadequately. Instead they should be seen as occasions for reviewing ownership, management, and making major adjustments to how the firm is set up.

I. Change in corporate strategy

A great deal of research in corporate strategy has been devoted to the question of diversification, with a particular emphasis on comparing the performance effects of related and unrelated diversification (where relatedness is a function of the extent to which the different businesses of the multibusiness firm share resources and markets).[4]

The study of why firms engage in corporate strategies of unrelated diversification despite the negative evidence on performance represents one of the few specific points of comparison between research in strategy and research in finance. Strategy explains the persistence of unrelated diversification in some cases by citing managerial competences in parenting, i.e., economies of scope in processes that can be brought to bear across businesses, such as finance, accounting, or planning.[5] Finance is more skeptical about managerial competences and invokes managerial power over decision-making and managerial rent seeking to the detriment of shareholders who do not need management to diversify portfolio risk on their behalf (in the publicly listed firm).[6] In the first approach, managerial competences are difficult to pinpoint and shareholders are not considered; in the second, management and shareholders have diametrically opposed interests. What if diversification in particular, and changes in corporate strategy in general, were analyzed in light of the interplay of the values among and between managers and shareholders instead?

Firms branch out into new businesses for reasons that include prospects for growth, access to resources, diversification of risk, *as well as* the desire of individuals to hold sway over more resources and earn more money. When a firm adds a new business to its portfolio, management's span of control is stretched and governance systems have to handle an increase in complexity. Depending on how the growth is financed, adding a new business may also imply adding new shareholders, or substituting existing shareholders with new shareholders. If the growth is not equity financed, the influence of creditors will be boosted. Conversely, selling off a business simplifies the task of corporate management, reduces the complexity of governance, and may permit a firm to concentrate the shareholding structure and retire creditors. In other words, whether additive or subtractive, changes in corporate strategy are likely to have a considerable impact on management, ownership, and governance. Difficulties arise when these impacts are not anticipated, and decision-makers have to improvise.

Change in corporate strategy can expose weaknesses in corporate governance

Consider the case of the entrepreneur who has been extremely successful in one line of business and attempts to transpose this success into a completely new field, when the opportunity arises. A typical example is that of the emerging market entrepreneur – be it in India, in Egypt, or in Brazil – who uses funds from their original business to get in on the ground floor of telecommunications or utilities or natural resources, as these industries are opened up to the private sector. The entrepreneur has the connections to get the first deals done quickly and the corporate infrastructure to hit the ground running. The trouble is that the new businesses also require new management skills and put strains on the existing corporate infrastructure, even if the entrepreneur has not had to have recourse to outside funding. Telecommunications, for instance, involves a time cycle of investment that is much longer and a process of coordination that is far more complicated than what the entrepreneur and their organization are likely to be used to. As long as things are going well and revenues grow at a faster pace than costs, this may not appear to matter. However, once growth slows or competition increases, the tensions in the system will be magnified. At this point, the entrepreneur typically goes for double or nothing, and since neither the management nor the governance system have been adapted to match the new complexity of the multibusiness firm, there is no structure to support them and no one to advise them (and eventually hold them back).[7]

Note that the case of the entrepreneur who adds a new business does not raise issues of managerial rent seeking or of unnecessary diversification – the entrepreneur is essentially managing and diversifying their own portfolio of assets. And yet, the change in corporate strategy is a challenge for the governance system of the firm. Adding a new business exposes any weaknesses in control and accountability, because it means dealing with new people, new processes, and new competitive risks. In the new business, the people cannot be managed in the same way (accountability), and the structure cannot be administered in the same way (control). The more the new business differs from the existing businesses in the portfolio, the greater the challenge it poses to governance.[8] In the excitement of the opportunity, entrepreneurs rarely take the link between strategy change and governance change into consideration. As a result, governance usually lags behind, and problems only become apparent with a considerable delay. Even then, the typical symptoms of governance problems (accounting discrepancies, overstepping of boundaries, disputes between managers over who is responsible for what, etc.) may be put off by the entrepreneur and their team as not fundamental to the business, and ignored. In our view, this is a serious mistake, for these symptoms mask problems that will burst into prominence when growth slows.

Point to watch: preparing for slowing growth

When a firm is growing at very high speed, few shareholders or managers are willing to sit down and think about corporate governance. On the one hand, time taken away from growing the business seems like time wasted; on the other hand, corporate governance and its attendant structures and procedures have the reputation of costing money and slowing firms down. The key to preparing for slowing growth is keeping a hand on the till and staying realistic about numbers. If sustaining high levels of growth is dependent on acquisitions panning out, key performers continuing to exceed expectations, or large clients or partners staying loyal, then the firm is vulnerable to a shock when growth slows. At the least, the aforementioned variables need to be very carefully monitored, all the more so if much of the growth is coming in new business areas or new geographies. Even better would be to build in early warning systems focused on the main vulnerabilities of rapid growth.

If other shareholders are involved or if the firm is publicly listed, the questions about governance are even more important. Take the situation (very common in many emerging markets) where the firm is publicly listed, but the founding entrepreneur (and their family) still owns a majority of the shares.[9] If changes in corporate strategy are likely to expose governance weaknesses and if they are also likely to lead to double or nothing efforts to recover in the event of poor performance, then minority shareholders have every reason to be worried about the addition of a new business, whatever its growth prospects. Not surprisingly, therefore, changes in corporate strategy have been at the origin of a number of recent struggles over the rights of minority shareholders.[10] Again, the question is not about the validity of the change in corporate strategy per se, but rather about the adequacy of the governance systems and, in the case of publicly listed firms, the consideration of the different interests of diverse shareholders. Changes in corporate strategy invariably raise governance and, in many cases, ownership issues. It is better to address these ex ante, before they turn into full-blown confrontations over the direction of the firm.

Point to watch: conflict over shareholder rights

When minority shareholders protest new growth strategies in a publicly listed, but majority owned firm, they are really exposing a conflict over who has the right to direct the firm and to what purpose. Diversifying the firm (further) by entering a new business may well be in the best interests of the founder or family that still has the lion's share of its assets tied up in the firm. In this case, the change in corporate strategy occurs to suit the needs of the largest shareholder and may well not be in the interests of other shareholders who can diversify their portfolios in the capital markets. If we look at strategy as the outcome of a political struggle among shareholders, as well as between shareholders and management, then this is not surprising. Minority shareholders who invest in firms where founding entrepreneurs or their families still hold sway cannot expect these firms to be led in the same way as firms without a large entrepreneur shareholder – they have to accept the advantages of this constellation with the disadvantages.

Change in corporate strategy as an opportunity for a renewal of governance

A change in corporate strategy can be an opportunity for rethinking both the governance and the ownership of the firm. When Mars, Inc., made Wm. Wrigley Jr. the largest acquisition in its almost one-hundred-year corporate history in 2008, for example, a great deal of thought went into the questions of structure and funding. On the one hand, it was decided to create a separate structure for Wrigley, in order to make sure that the chewing gum business would stand on its own feet. Even more important, however, given the size of the acquisition, was the decision on funding. As a fourth-generation family firm, Mars values its freedom very highly; in fact, freedom has been enshrined as one of the Five Principles of the firm since 1977. Because of its size, the Wrigley acquisition had the potential to compromise the financial freedom of Mars. In order to be able to do the deal on the firm's own terms, the family and senior management decided to draw on a form of financing that was especially suited to their needs: debt and equity participation from investor Warren Buffett, to be paid back exclusively from the earnings of Wrigley. Buffett shares the business philosophy of the family, long-term strategies over short-term moves, and, crucially for Mars, agreed to a ten-year deal that did not ransom the future of the legacy businesses. In this way, Mars could stay faithful to its principles and still adapt its ownership model to fit the change in corporate strategy.[11]

Hilti, the foundation-owned construction equipment giant first described in Chapter 3, also considers changes in corporate strategy in light of the governance challenges they pose. Michael Hilti, former chairman of the board and head of the family foundation, explains that new board members are chosen for their experience in the business and technology areas that the firm *plans to enter in the next five years*, not for their knowledge of the firm's current businesses.[12] In this way, discussions at the board level are informed by deep knowledge about the firm's future perspectives and not dominated by past practice. We will have more to say about board composition in Chapter 8, but it is worth pointing out that taking the future into account in this manner represents a powerful way of preparing the governance of a firm for the challenges of entering new businesses and may help avoid the failures of understanding described in the previous section.

Changes in corporate strategy: effects on ownership

Changes in corporate strategy have an impact on the firm's liquidity. On the one hand, a change in corporate strategy will reduce (or augment) the amount of cash available; just as important, because it ties up resources (or frees up resources), a change in corporate strategy will mark a change in the firm's time horizon. Branching out into a new business is a commitment and an investment in the future that makes it harder to turn around and sell the firm; selling off businesses, on the other hand, increases visibility and makes the firm as a whole easier to sell. As soon as there are multiple shareholders with different values, there is therefore going to be some disagreement about *any* changes in corporate strategy. Whereas entrepreneurs, with internal values linked to the growth of the firm are more likely to favor investing in new businesses, traders and activists with external values tied to market performance measures will come down on the side of selling off businesses and trimming the corporate strategy of what they regard as nonessentials.[13] At the very least, therefore, a change in corporate strategy has the potential to affect the shareholding structure, giving more weight to shareholders with internal values or shareholders with external values, depending on the choice made.

As we have seen in Chapter 1, entrepreneurs and activists don't just react to changes in corporate strategy, they seek to actively shape corporate strategy. Thus, investments in new businesses may come at the behest of entrepreneurs, while divestments may occur at the insistence of activists. In these cases, change in corporate strategy does not occur for "purely strategic" reasons, but clearly reflects and furthers the interests of (a particular group of) shareholders. For shareholders who have a substantial proportion of their wealth tied up in a firm (i.e., family or foundation), a change of corporate strategy toward diversification also represents a diversification of that shareholder's own investment portfolio and may indeed be the only way for them to diversify. This reasoning applies regardless of whether the firm is listed or not, and many firms with large single shareholders or shareholder groups are in fact relatively diversified, even more so if based in emerging markets with illiquid capital markets that do not permit large shareholders to achieve a satisfactory degree of financial diversification.[14]

By contrast, activists and traders generally prefer narrowly focused corporate strategies; as finance theory demonstrates, given liquid capital markets, and given relatively small investments in any single firm, shareholders can diversify by themselves.[15] As discussed in Chapter 1, firms with diversified corporate strategies have become so unattractive to traders in recent years that activists explicitly target them. Activists such as the Hermes Focus Funds or the Governance for Owners Focus Funds seek to prod diversified firms into unwinding their collection of businesses, so that the run of the mill trader will once again buy the firms' shares.[16] Despite harboring different views about the value of diversification, however, entrepreneurs and activists rarely come into direct conflict. This is because activists prefer to target firms that are not protected by entrepreneurs with their own reasons for diversification; when they do target such firms, they typically meet with great and sometimes insurmountable opposition from shareholders with internal values. In firms with dispersed shareholdings, it is much easier to build shareholder coalitions against management and obtain the desired changes.

Who decides on a change in corporate strategy?

As we have seen, changes in corporate strategy are not purely economic decisions, but rather result from the interplay of shareholders and managers. In fact, a change in corporate strategy is an excellent test of who is really in charge of making decisions in the firm. In the case of an entrepreneur who owns their own firm, this question does not need to be asked: for all intents and purposes, the firm is an extension of the individual. However, as soon as several actors (shareholders and managers) are involved, the values and the methods of these actors are likely to conflict, and proposed changes in corporate strategy will be a testing ground for carrying out these conflicts. Activists, for example, are likely to prefer corporate strategy moves toward simplification, whereas entrepreneurs may have specific reasons to support diversification (see Table 1.3); analogously, adopters among executive management will try to steer the firm toward a corporate strategy that satisfies current market demands, while transformers may insist on an idiosyncratic approach that goes against current market expectations (see Table 2.3). If power is dispersed, then the firm's ultimate choice of corporate strategy is very hard to predict – it will depend on how the game of influencing among shareholders and managers plays out. A change in corporate strategy toward one point of view and away from the others indicates a (temporary) winner in the continuous struggle over who decides.[17]

Case in point: globalization and corporate governance

The decision to globalize (effectively a decision for geographic diversification) represents one of the most significant changes in corporate strategy. In deciding to globalize, a firm moves to capitalize on the opportunity for business without borders and chooses to view the world as a single market space (while taking national differences into account). This implies that administrative systems, business practices, and indeed management mindsets need to be adapted to a new, much broader conception of the firm and its competitive environment. What about corporate governance – is globalization corporate governance neutral or does it also lead to changes in how the firm is set up, and to modifications in the roles of shareholders and management?

From the point of view of corporate governance, the globalizing firm is exposed to two primary forces for change: institutional and informational. By globalizing, the firm in effect becomes part of multiple institutional contexts, and, because the firm views the world as a single market space, it cannot favor some contexts over others. As a result, the firm comes under pressure to adopt rules and procedures of corporate governance that are universally recognized or meet generally accepted standards of accounting and law.[18] To the extent that globalization necessitates or attracts new global capital, the pressure to conform to such standards is extended to questions of reporting, shareholder rights, and board member independence. One would therefore expect that national or firm-specific characteristics of corporate governance tend to decline over time in globalizing firms, at the firm level of analysis. However, how governance changes with globalization depends on the history of the individual firm.[19]

Globalization also implies increased informational complexity – in terms of institutional contexts, of course, but also in terms of the production processes, customer preferences, and competitive environments. This increase in informational complexity makes it much more difficult for board members and existing (domestic) shareholders to keep tabs on and evaluate what is happening in the firm. The actors who do have access to and requisite understanding of the information associated with globalization are the senior managers. This is why globalization tends to make managers less substitutable and increase their decision-making power, while reducing the power of domestic shareholders and other local stakeholders, at least for as long as the globalization process is successful.[20]

In light of these considerations, the decision to globalize is not to be taken lightly, especially by domestic shareholders. The economic imperative and the chance to build a sustainable global franchise need to be weighed against the potential loss of governance specificity and decision-making power. Small shareholders may not have much say in the matter, but "core" shareholders with a substantial stake in the firm and internal values, such as governments, foundations, and families, stand to lose a substantial proportion of their ability to shape the future of the firm. Is there any evidence that core shareholders recognize this and try to preserve their prerogatives against the forces for change unleashed by globalization?

In the following, we discuss the relationship between globalization and corporate governance in three well-known firms, representing the principal different types of core shareholders: Renault (the fourth-largest automaker in the world; state as core shareholder); Fresenius (the world leader in renal care; foundation as core shareholder), and Bombardier (the world leader in trains and mid-size passenger aircraft; family as core shareholder). The analysis is based on interviews conducted with decision-makers, company archives, and secondary data.[21] In all three cases, a variety of minor, separately managed international activities preceded globalization, and enough time has elapsed between the launch of the globalization process and the time of writing of this book to now make meaningful statements about the impact of globalization on corporate governance (1999 for Renault; 1995 for Fresenius; and 1989 for Bombardier).

Renault launched its globalization with the signing of a strategic alliance with troubled Japanese automaker Nissan in 1999. With the alliance agreement, Renault acquired 33 percent of the shares of Nissan and the right to appoint the senior management, including the new CEO of Nissan, Carlos Ghosn. By 2002, Nissan was profitable again and could consummate the equity partnership, taking on 15 percent ownership of Renault, while Renault raised its stake in Nissan to 44 percent. In 2005, Carlos Ghosn replaced Louis Schweitzer at the head of Renault and has since been CEO to both firms, leading the alliance's expansion into India, China, and Russia. After going from strength to strength, and even being considered as a potential savior for General Motors, the Renault/Nissan alliance was hit hard by the downturn of 2008–2009, and Renault had to call on the French state for an infusion of €3 billion in cash in order to return to health.

According to Louis Schweitzer, CEO of Renault, "the French state did not intervene in the alliance discussions with Nissan";[22] it approved of the firm's plans to globalize. Since then, the French state has allowed its ownership stake in Renault to steadily decline, from 46 percent in 1999 to 15.3 percent in 2005, but continues to appoint two directors to the board of Renault, has provided project-based funding (2009), and played a role in defusing the spy scandal that embroiled the firm in 2010–2011. While it is clear the power of management and particularly of CEO Carlos Ghosn has increased significantly in the years since globalization (Carlos Ghosn is also chairman of the board of Renault), it is also evident that the French state has maintained a considerable amount of influence in the company as evidenced by its board appointees and funding. Moreover, the ownership structure of Renault remains "unusual" in the sense that the major shareholders besides France and Nissan include several other large French institutions with close ties to the French state. In other words, France has remained a shareholder in Renault throughout the process of globalization, and offered critical support to the firm's very special bi-national model of governance and management.

Globalization at Fresenius really got under way when Dr. Gerd Krick took over as CEO in 1992. He built a new management team around him and reorganized the company before shocking the renal care industry with the purchase of US-based National Medical Care (NMC) in 1995, a company that was considerably larger than Fresenius. In part to pay for the purchase of NMC, the largest of the Fresenius group companies, Fresenius Medical Care, listed on the New York Stock Exchange. Over the more than fifteen years since that daring purchase, Fresenius has also globalized its three other businesses and today operates in over a hundred countries on six continents. During this time, the ownership stake of the Else Kröner-Fresenius foundation has declined from 58 percent to 29 percent, and the foundation today has only one representative on the board of Fresenius (the chairman of the foundation, Dieter Schwenk, a lawyer). The foundation is still appreciated by management as a stable, long-term shareholder (as part of what the 2010 annual report calls a "well-balanced shareholder structure" with over forty institutional shareholders),[23] but the only descendant of the founder's family has been removed from the supervisory board of the firm and the board of the foundation (2008) and all preference shares have been converted to ordinary shares (2011). Today, the foundation exerts no discernable influence on strategic decision-making in the firm.

At Bombardier, globalization started in earnest in the late 1980s and early 1990s, with a series of acquisitions in Europe and North America that took advantage of the poor financial condition of a number of traditional national champions in trains and passenger aircraft. Thanks to advanced management methods, particularly in manufacturing and in key processes such as bidding for contracts, the firm grew apace and became a poster child for industrial revitalization on a global scale. In 1999, finally, a nonfamily executive, Robert Brown, replaced the founder's son-in-law, Laurent Beaudoin, as the CEO, the first nonfamily member to ever lead the firm on a full-time basis. Brown had the misfortune to preside over the firm during the crisis in the aircraft industry occasioned by 9/11 and the ensuing slowdown and was initially replaced by another nonfamily executive, Paul Tellier. Bombardier had overextended itself in both trains and aircraft and could not weather the storm without the sale of the recreational vehicle business that had been the origin of the firm's growth and a fresh infusion of capital from the founding family (2003). This marked a turning point for the firm, with the subsequent installation of Laurent Beaudoin's son, Pierre, first in a newly created office of the president together with his father (2004) and then as the CEO (2008). With the resumption of executive duties, the family renewed its commitment to the firm. During all the time that has passed since the launch of globalization at Bombardier and the turmoil of the first decade of the twenty-first century, the Bombardier-Beaudoin family maintained its position as core shareholder with majority voting rights (thanks to dual class shares) and the chief positions on the board of directors. This is what allowed the family to take back the reins of leadership when growth stalled and creditors called for additional funds.

What do these three cases reveal about the relationship between globalization (change in corporate strategy) and changes in corporate governance? First of all, we can say that, counter to expectations and with a minimum of twelve years passed since the launch of globalization, in all three firms the core shareholder has maintained some degree of influence on decision-making and corporate governance remains "unusual." This is to be expected when the substitutability of the core shareholder is low. The cases do suggest that globalization affects management power and institutional conformity in the expected direction, but that these effects are contingent on the strength of personal and structural ties of the core shareholder to the firm: in Bombardier, where the family always maintained a close personal connection to the firm and dual class shares perpetuated their dominance of the shareholding structure, the effects are weakest;

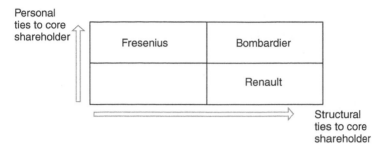

Figure 5.1 The publicly listed firm with a core shareholder: personal ties and structural ties.

in Fresenius, where personal ties to the foundation are tenuous and the foundation does not have enough weight in the shareholding structure to oppose management and other shareholders (primarily international funds), the effects are strongest. The effect of globalization on corporate governance depends on the personal involvement and structural positioning of core shareholders. As Figure 5.1 shows, where ties to managers are mainly personal (Fresenius) or structural (Renault), managers are strongest and governance has changed the most; at both Fresenius (impending retirement of chairman) and Renault (vulnerability to activist shareholder attack), the hold of the core shareholder is weakened.

As the three cases show, a significant change in corporate strategy like globalization leads to pressure for corresponding changes in management and ownership. However, decision-makers, in this case core shareholders, can resist this pressure for change, and put mechanisms in place to prevent or soften changes in management and ownership. If core shareholders seek to maintain their influence, is this "good" or "bad" for the firm? This question cannot be answered in the abstract. Our view is that strategic choices (i.e., globalization) are always *also* political, i.e., in the interests of one group of stakeholders and, possibly, against the interests of others. Institutional and informational considerations lead to the prediction that globalization enhances the position of managers (more institutional conformity, more power); this may or may not be good for the firm.

A change in corporate strategy necessarily implies rethinking the roles of ownership and management.

Change in corporate strategy – conclusion

Whether to invest in a new business or to divest an existing business, to diversify across products or markets (globalization), changes in corporate strategy invariably put pressure on ownership, management, and governance systems. As we have shown, this pressure can be resisted, and it is perhaps most accurate to think of changes in corporate strategy as prime occasions for rethinking the balance of power between ownership and management and for questioning the adequacy of existing governance systems. In other words, changes in corporate strategy are never corporate governance neutral and should never be looked at in isolation, in purely economic terms. In addition to thinking about risk and return, shareholders, managers, and their advisors need to consider whose interests will be served most by any change in corporate strategy and reflect upon how to protect the firm against unwanted side effects.

II. Change in business strategy

Unlike corporate strategy, business strategy is rarely linked to corporate governance concerns and does not appear to raise any immediate questions for ownership. This is because business strategy is about positioning and resource allocation in a given industry or market and takes place at a level of specificity that ostensibly does not affect governance or ownership. Whereas a change in corporate strategy takes the firm in a different direction, a change in business strategy implies an adjustment, an increase, or a reduction of commitment to a given course of action: changing how the firm plays a particular game (business), rather than changing the game. Deciding how the game is played is traditionally the preserve of (nonowner) management.[24]

Should governance and ownership be concerned with changes in business strategy? The history of the financial crisis associated with subprime mortgages (2007–2009) suggests that changes in business strategy can and do have significant effects on the long-term health of a firm. For the investment banks that suffered most from the collapse of the subprime market – Lehman Brothers, Bear Stearns, Dillon Read (as part of UBS), etc. – proprietary trading was not a new business and neither was securitization. What brought about these firms' downfalls was the business strategy decision to place bigger and bigger bets in the same business. In other words, and without changing the corporate strategy portfolio, management decided to increase the specific risk associated with the business of proprietary trading. However limited in scope and difficult to explain to nonspecialists, this decision put the entire firm at risk.

One might argue that this kind of increase in business-specific risk is particular to the world of financial institutions. In fact, nonfinancials also take business strategy decisions with far-reaching implications: major acquisitions in the same line of business in pharmaceuticals, fast-moving consumer goods, or industrial products; platform shifts in consumer electronics or computer hardware; refocusing on a different category of client in service businesses, etc. In the single-business firm such changes of business strategy can have far-reaching effects, of course, but even in the case of the multibusiness firm, there is the potential to fundamentally alter long-term prospects – just think of Cadbury Schweppes' expensive and ill-advised attempt to reinforce its American beverages business with the acquisition of Snapple in 2000. Weakened by several acquisitions that cost too much and could not be profitably integrated, Cadbury Schweppes was forced to spin off its beverage business at the worst time (listing of the newly formed Dr Pepper Snapple group in 2008), and the remaining confectionery business became easy prey for Kraft.[25] As this and other examples show, it is naïve to expect that corporate governance and ownership will not be affected by significant changes in the specific risk associated with one or more businesses, in *any* kind of industry environment.

In our research, we find that ownership tends to react more rapidly to changes in business strategy than corporate governance. In publicly listed companies, analysts are quick to put the spotlight on changes in business strategy and funds that focus on particular kinds of strategies or invest by choosing among industry rivals (i.e., long/short funds) move even faster.[26] This has the effect of changing the shareholding structure, to include more of those traders who favor the new business strategy. It is a matter of empirical debate whether traders follow a change in business strategy or, in some cases, precipitate the change. In any case, in publicly listed companies, a change in business strategy is not shareholder neutral.

Point to watch: management fads

Where do management fads come from, and do the equity markets play a role in their propagation? Generally, new management ideas and new strategies are the result of successful experimentation by a few leading companies. In the case of the publicly listed firm, traders are quick to spot these innovations and to reward them by buying the shares of the leading innovators. This puts the pressure of market expectations on comparable firms to follow suit; if they do not, they will be asked by analysts to explain why. Over time, observers and consultants add to the pressure for conformity by writing about and systematizing the hot new approach. Indeed, many firms will actually pay consultants to help them to adopt the fad, just to be sure that they are doing the right thing. Once the excitement blows over, those firms that did not have good business reasons to adopt the fad and did not have the management skills to make it pay off quickly enough often become the target of activists intent on undoing whatever steps have been taken in the direction of the fad and removing management. The entire process is depicted in Figure 5.2 below.

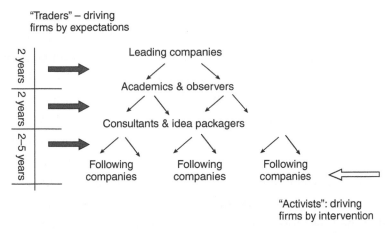

Figure 5.2 The role of shareholders in management fads.

As we have seen in Section I of this chapter, the corporate governance systems of the firm are often slow to adapt. In part this is due to the infrequent periodicity of the principal institutions of corporate governance, the annual general meeting and the board meetings; in addition, the complexity of the procedures of corporate governance often contributes to making them inflexible. It should come as no surprise, therefore, to note that the corporate governance systems of most investment banks did not adapt to the dramatically changed risk profile of their trading businesses until long after the resulting financial crisis had already played out. They have been changed now, putting considerably more attention on the measurement and control of risk, as a direct response to the changes in business strategy that contributed to the crisis.[27] In all likelihood, however, change in corporate governance systems will continue to lag behind changes in business (and corporate) strategy.

Different types of changes in business strategy

Leaving the question of how strategy is made aside, the field of business strategy is traditionally divided between the question of competitive positioning (industry analysis) and the question of resource accumulation and exploitation (resource-based view of the firm).[28] The former focuses attention on the environment and looks at the business from the outside in, while the latter takes an inside-out approach in describing the skills that the business needs to succeed in the marketplace. With these two frameworks as guideposts for thinking about business strategy, there are countless permutations for change: new market/new resource, old market/new resource, new market/old resource, etc., with multiple markets and multiple resources to work through. Clearly, there is no way to cover all of the possibilities. Instead, we will focus on one of the variables that is of primary interest to ownership and governance: the increase (or decrease) of risk implied by a change in business strategy. As depicted in Figure 5.3, the risk of a change in business strategy is a function of both the uncertainty of markets and the difficulty of managing the required resources.

If we take the decision of (a number of) US investment banks to increase proprietary trading in mortgage-backed assets as an example, we can see that the challenge for both ownership and governance lies in correctly assessing the actual risk of the change in business strategy. As long as mortgage-backed assets were rated AAA investments, market uncertainty could be classified as low; and, as long as proprietary trading in these assets could be deemed to fall within the scope of business as usual, management difficulty could also be classified as low. As events transpired, it became clear that market uncertainty was very high and that many of the investment banks did not have the necessary management skills to oversee and assess all the different kinds of new assets on their books. In terms of the framework presented here, a change in business strategy that had been presented as low risk, turned out to belong to the category of highest risk. If we now recall that the CEOs of many (investment) banks had publicly promised to achieve significant increases in return on equity (ROE) through trading activities in a

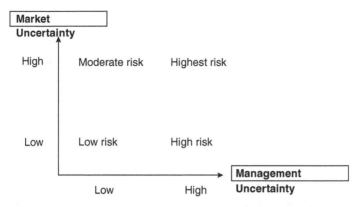

Figure 5.3 Determining the risk of a change in business strategy.

very short time (i.e., from 15 percent to 25 percent in two years, as in the case of Deutsche Bank),[29] then it becomes clear that the move to strengthen proprietary trading in mortgage-backed securities represented a major change in business strategy. Some shareholders, it would seem, caught on to what was happening and jumped aboard to ride the new strategy to new share price highs. Too many, however – and this includes the board of directors – failed to gauge the full impact of the change in business strategy.

The difficulty of implementing new strategies[30]

Success in the implementation of new strategies continues to elude many firms. Both the scholarly literature and the business press have consistently reported that a large proportion of strategic decisions do not reach their objectives because of a failure to implement.[31] In the special case of publicly listed firms, the perceived need to attract traders can be a powerful motivating force for some executives to develop new strategies that promise greater returns;[32] traders are looking for fresh reasons to buy the stock and care more about how the financial markets react to the new strategy than about the feasibility of the new strategy.[33] Often, the new strategies developed to attract traders depend (for successful implementation) on complex processes of which the firm has relatively little experience. For example, management of trading risk (in the case of a bank extending its activities in derivatives markets), delivery of business consulting (in the case of a maker of products seeking to offer solutions), and global coordination (in the case of a formerly public utility attempting to globalize).[34] In effect, catering to traders, executive management may pursue new strategies that their organizations do not have the skills to implement.

Where there is little experience and the processes involved in making the new strategies work are complex, understanding about the relationship between firm resources and competitive advantage will be subject to a considerable degree of causal ambiguity. Research in strategic management has shown that this is the kind of context in which middle managers play key roles as repositories of knowledge about what is feasible and what is not feasible, and executive management has difficulty interpreting the information they receive.[35] This gap in the utilization of knowledge can be explained by observing that top management and middle management have different ways of seeing the world and hence do not understand the relationship between firm resources and competitive advantage in the same way.[36]

Strategy implementation research is grounded in a decision-making view that divides the process of making strategy into distinct stages: before a decision (strategy formulation) and after a decision (strategy implementation). Although this view has been criticized as unnecessarily rigid and divorced from the reality of many firms, especially in fast-moving environments, it continues to serve as the basis for a great deal of influential work in the field.[37] Consistent with this view, research on strategy implementation failure focuses on the study of strategic decisions and looks for the sources of failure in both the processes of ex ante decision-making and post hoc implementation. In the literature, difficulties in the implementation of new strategies are thus traced to errors in decision-making and insufficiencies in change management: decision-making processes that do not take all relevant information about the environment into account leading to poor quality decisions;[38] and incomplete communication from executive management and inadequate adaptation of structures causing poor understanding in the organization and an inability to overcome resistance to change.[39]

Studies that document the extent of strategy implementation failure also follow this schema.[40] Failure is traced to limiting the search for solutions (ex ante) and imposing decisions on the organization (post hoc), or, alternatively, failure results from inadequate planning (ex ante) or insufficient prioritization (post hoc). What is remarkable in these studies and indeed in many other analyses of strategy implementation failure is the fact that the feasibility of the strategy being pursued is not taken into consideration. Presumably, the feasibility of the strategy, defined in terms of the decision-makers' perceived understanding of the issue and the decision-makers' perceived capability to resolve the issue, plays a critical role in determining the success or the failure of implementation.[41] According to the resource-based view of the firm, a strategy that is better understood and better aligned with the firm's core skills will be easier to implement, while a strategy that takes the firm farther afield will be more difficult to successfully put in place.[42]

In the broader literature of organizational change, a distinction is made between radical change and incremental change. Whereas radical change implies a qualitative difference in how the firm is organized, incremental change means working within the existing rules and relationships.[43] Clearly, radical change is more difficult to pull off, but while incremental change is always feasible, radical change may or may not be, depending on how the firm is positioned towards the specific change being considered.[44] Hambrick and D'Aveni's notion of domain initiative – the degree to which a firm changes its products and markets – is helpful in gaining a finer-grained understanding of the strategy implementation issues we are considering. In the organizational change literature, failure of organizations is associated either with too little change (inertia) or too much change (too often and/or too far afield in terms of domain initiative).[45] Again, we need to interpose feasibility – whether or not extreme domain initiative is successful necessarily hinges on understanding and capability, at the level of the decision-makers, of course, but, perhaps even more importantly, at the level of the middle management that has to make the change work.[46]

This discussion highlights the need to consider feasibility in a more nuanced manner. Feasible or not feasible from the point of view of decision-makers (i.e., executive management), or from the point of view of middle management, or as an organizational concept to be considered at the same level of analysis as capabilities in the resource-based view of the firm? The observation that executive management in publicly listed firms, focusing on traders, may attempt unfeasible new strategies has different implications, depending at what level of analysis feasibility is defined. Executive management may simply have a very different view of what is feasible and what is not feasible from middle management. However, when executive management goes ahead with a new strategy that the organization does not have the understanding or the capability to execute successfully, there may also be other reasons, either personal or external to the firm.[47]

Knowledge about the feasibility of a new strategy, defined as perceived understanding and perceived capability, is not limited to executive management. Where there is little experience, and the processes involved in making the new strategies work are complex, understanding about the relationship between firm resources and competitive advantage will be subject to a considerable degree of causal ambiguity. In other words, different managers and different levels of management will have different perspectives on the why (understanding) and the how (capability) of a new strategy. Put simply, middle managers have close ties to reality on the ground, allowing them to directly relate actions and consequences, even under conditions of novelty and complexity; executive management sees a different, filtered slice of the world and responds to different contextual cues, and these differences can lead to very different conclusions when there is considerable uncertainty about the relationship between cause and effect.

The differences in how executive management and middle management make sense of the world around them when causal ambiguity is high can in turn be traced to cognitive differences and socio-structural differences between the two levels of managers. Following in the footsteps of the Carnegie School, research on managerial cognition has shown that executive management and middle management work with different kinds of information and focus their attention on different aspects of the firm.[48] In the case in which new strategies are proposed that take the firm out of its domain, these differences are likely to be especially significant to how executive management and middle managers assess feasibility – executive management sifting through aggregate reports and focusing on externals like market and competitive data, middle management working with experiences from their immediate surroundings and focusing on internals such as plant utilization figures and concrete personnel questions. Looking at a strategy that is novel and complex to implement from opposite angles, executive management and middle management are not likely to arrive at the same conclusions about feasibility.

Less prominent in the literature than cognitive differences between executive management and middle management, socio-structural differences revolving around interest and identity also contribute to the gap in how knowledge in the firm is used.[49] In effect, executive management and middle management play in different compensation and employment markets and belong to different social identity groups. Whereas executive management measures itself against the top management of other firms of similar size and has its compensation structured accordingly, the pay scale and market for middle management are essentially internal, centered on the performance of the function or the unit.[50] As a result, the interests of executive management and the interests of middle management are likely to diverge. Different interests lead to and are reinforced by a sense of belonging to different social identity groups. Executive managers are at home with the executive managers of other firms of similar importance, often in an international context, while middle managers typically remain local, rooted in their communities and in their professional specializations.[51] These socio-structural differences function as barriers between executive management and middle management and get in the way of the strategic discourse. They may be talking about the same new strategy, but in what amounts to different languages.

Point to watch: stock market speak

In publicly listed firms, top management tends to spend a great deal of time talking to and working with the financial community – shareholders, investment analysts, and financial journalists. In fact, for many firms, the time top management devotes to working with the financial community has increased dramatically, to the detriment of time spent with employees. Quite naturally, therefore, many top managers have adopted the language of the stock market, not only in their dealings with the financial community, but also in addressing their own employees. It is not uncommon to hear top managers speak to the staff almost exclusively in terms of overall revenue and profitability targets, broad strategic positioning, and nostrums about the need to transform and become more dynamic. As a result, we observe an increasing disconnect between top management and the rest of the firm, a disconnect that can only be overcome if top management explicitly makes the link between the language of the financial community and the language of operations.[52]

When pronounced, cognitive differences and socio-structural differences between top management and middle management can help explain the knowledge utilization gap that is at the heart of unfeasible new strategies. Of course, not all of the actors will attribute the pursuit of unfeasible new strategies and subsequent strategy implementation failures to these differences. However, if some of the actors and, just as importantly, some of the stakeholders recognize the dysfunctional effects, those firms that build better bridges between executive management and middle management should reap the benefits in terms of strategy implementation success, and ultimately, financial performance.

Adapting governance for the impact of a change in business strategy

Although it is not the norm, it is possible to adapt governance systems to the requirements imposed by an important change in business strategy in a relatively short amount of time. Nomura's effort in this regard following the firm's 2008 acquisitions of the Asia Pacific, European, and Indian operations of defunct Lehman Brothers provides a noteworthy example. The deal was made with the idea of strengthening Nomura's international investment banking and trading businesses. Recognizing that the acquisitions of significant parts and over 8,000 people of the old Lehman Brothers would pose great challenges in terms of getting different national cultures and contrasting firm styles to work together and therefore represent a high risk proposition in terms of management difficulty, decision-makers at Nomura took a number of significant steps to modify their governance systems.

First, they worked out new incentive systems for all of their employees, with regional variations. In Europe, Nomura today looks a lot like Lehman used to; in Japan, employees were given a choice between Lehman-style packages and Nomura-style packages, essentially a tradeoff between compensation and job security. Second, they significantly strengthened the board of the holding company. Building on the practice of installing senior independent directors already established in 2003, the firm in 2010 brought in its first two non-Japanese independents, the former chairman of British Airways, Lord Colin Marshall, and the former chief executive of the London Stock Exchange Group, Dame Clara Furse (followed in 2011 by a third non-Japanese independent, Michael Lim Choo San, who has held senior positions at PricewaterhouseCoopers and in the Singaporean government). Unlike the boards of most other Japanese companies, the board of Nomura Holdings is organized around committees, including an audit committee, where the independents are in the majority. Lastly, the company significantly increased the weight of the audit function, giving it representation on the board, supported by two full-time nonexecutives and an office of the audit committee.[53]

Taken together, these corporate governance reforms represented a significant and timely response to the altered risk profile produced by the Lehman acquisition. As it happens, the governance changes described here could not prevent Nomura from suffering large losses subsequent to the financial crisis; like others in the industry, they have seen trading in the market decline precipitously since 2008, resulting in significant losses for the firm. In addition, a domestic (i.e., Japanese, non-Lehman) insider trading scandal has also hurt Nomura, leading to the resignation of the CEO and the COO in

2012. It is not clear if the corporate governance reforms enacted with the Lehman purchase have been effective in addressing the significant amount of new risk taken on. However, we can say that decision-makers at the firm recognized that a change in business strategy as major as that represented by the Lehman acquisition required an equivalent adjustment to the corporate governance systems, and the relative speed of Nomura's responses to its current travails suggests that the governance changes that were enacted have gained some traction.[54]

Change in business strategy – change in management

Whether the people at the top are old or new, a change in business strategy will lead to the hiring of new people at various management levels, as the firm discovers that it does not have all the management skills needed to make the new strategy work. As a matter of course, therefore, a change in business strategy leads to changes in the composition of the management team over time (a change that happens faster if the new strategy involves growth by acquisition, as in the case of Nomura). As new people come in, methods and goals also change, and corporate governance systems are put to the test.

Consider Nokia's efforts to revitalize its mobile phone business in response to the overwhelming success of Apple's iPhone. After years of unsuccessfully trying to play technological catch-up with its smart phone rivals, the firm's board of directors decided in 2010 to switch gears. The first step in that shift was the hiring of a new CEO from the outside, Stephen Elop, formerly of Microsoft. Under Elop, Nokia moved swiftly to sign a strategic alliance with Microsoft in February, 2011, abandoning the Symbian operating system it had pushed for so long in favor of Windows.[55] Not only did the firm hire a new CEO and change its business strategy, it also changed the very basis upon which it was going to compete. From a corporate governance point of view, pinning the firm's hopes on a single strategic alliance is an entirely new proposition, and it is not clear whether the firm has prepared adequately. What is clear is that the change of management that went along with the board's decision to change the strategy of the mobile phone business has put the firm in the entirely new position of depending on a (erstwhile) competitor for its long-term survival.

In Nokia's case, the change in senior management was explicitly intended to accelerate the strategic decision to reorient its smart phone business toward the Microsoft operating system. In other cases, decision-makers underestimate the consequences of the changes in management that come about as a result of the decision to adapt their business strategies. Managers ostensibly brought in merely to implement new strategies may well turn out to have ideas of their own, along the lines described in Chapter 2: thus, an adopter will seek to revise the strategy, if it does not suit their understanding of market expectations, while an entrepreneur will always try to put their own stamp on the strategy. In other words, shareholders and directors contemplating a change of business strategy need to consider the implications for management ex ante, before making investment decisions.

Change in business strategy – conclusion

Both in the academic literature and in the practice of management, change in business strategy is rarely associated with questions of ownership and governance. As we have shown here, change in business strategy implies a change in business-specific risk and can therefore have significant ramifications for both ownership and governance. In today's fast-moving environments, firms are called upon to regularly review and update their business strategies; indeed, in highly competitive contexts, they are exhorted to innovate their way out of the intense rivalries that lead to price erosion and destroy profitability. We argue that the efforts to change business strategy need to be examined in light of their effects on ownership and governance. Especially where a change in management is involved, a change in business strategy may have effects that are too extensive to be left to management alone. However context specific and technical in nature, business strategy change should not be looked at in isolation, but rather decided upon in full consideration of the potential impact on the firm's systems of corporate governance.

Change in strategy – change in ownership, change in management

As explained in this chapter, a change in corporate strategy or a change in business strategy can have far-reaching effects on corporate governance, potentially bringing about changes in the shareholder structure and in the management of the firm. Depending on what kind of shareholders are mobilized by the new strategy and what kinds of managers are chosen to implement the new strategy, the strategy itself may be altered, in line with the dynamics described in Chapters 1 to 4. As more easily substitutable shareholders and managers replace less easily substitutable shareholders and managers, for example, a move towards following market trends is reinforced. By contrast, a new strategy that attracts less substitutable shareholders and managers strengthens an idiosyncratic approach. In effect, changes in strategy and changes in ownership and management form a feedback loop that determines the direction of the firm over

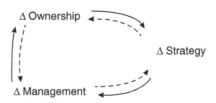

Figure 5.4 The ownership, management, and strategy feedback loop.

time (see Figure 5.4). This feedback loop is only broken when there is a fundamental shift in the balance of power among and between shareholders and managers. The following chapters explore under what conditions the balance of power in the firm tends to persist, even in the face of a shift in economic realities.

SIX

Despite failure, no change in ownership, management, or strategy

Why do firms change ownership, management, or strategy? One of the most significant drivers of change in business is failure. Failure, that is to say failure to meet performance expectations, is at the origin of many, if not all, of the changes we have discussed in this book: changes in ownership, because the original shareholders have run out of money or patience; changes in management, because the executives in place are unable to give the organization direction; and changes in strategy, because the firm or the business is poorly positioned to cope with the competition.[1] Of course, change is also driven by generational transition (i.e., succession of ownership or management) and anticipation (i.e., planning in strategy or management), but, in a market economy, the threat of failure is always an important spark for action. And yet, in some cases, ownership, management, and strategy do not change, *despite failure*. Thus, there are firms that decline progressively and lose money for years, without triggering strategic change. There are also firms that experience significant discrete setbacks without showing any apparent reaction. These cases of no change seemingly contradict the underlying argument that changes in ownership, management, and strategy, are adaptive measures necessary for ensuring the long-term health of the firm.

When do ownership, management, and strategy resist change, despite failure? From the point of view developed in this book, we identify two basic no change scenarios: (a) when power over decision-making is concentrated in one person; and (b) when the powers over decision-making are in a stalemate, and no decisions can be taken.[2]

I. Concentration of power and change

The founder-run firm constitutes the prototypical case of concentrated power: ownership, management, and strategy are rolled into one and all answer to the same person.[3] As long as the founder-run firm does not experience setbacks that threaten its existence, it can carry on without adapting ownership, management, or strategy. This may be suboptimal from an economic point of view, merely delaying the final collapse, but it is a standard feature of many founder-run firms that get into trouble. Power over decision-making rests with the founder, and if they do not see fit to make changes, none will occur.

Power over decision-making can effectively be concentrated in one person or one economic actor even in very large, publicly quoted firms. Examples are the all-powerful chief executive or the dominant core shareholder (family, foundation, or state) who can maintain their hold on ownership, management, and strategy no matter how difficult the situation of the firm. In some cases, this kind of hold over the firm extends even beyond the person's (or actor's) actual mandate. Thus, at Korean electronics giant Samsung the voluntary resignation of Chairman Lee from the firm in 2008 (to take moral responsibility for legal questions related to the involvement of his family in corporate structures related to Samsung) and the concurrent departure of a number of senior executives inaugurated a two-year period during which the firm effectively was treading water. Lee's influence (as the major shareholder and father figure of the firm) over the interim decision-makers of the firm was so great that major investment decisions were delayed until his return to full functions in 2010, despite the fact that the firm faced important competitive challenges in several of its main businesses.[4]

Clearly, separation of powers is at issue in cases such as these. One person or economic actor holds all the strings of ownership, management, and strategy, and is so powerful that seemingly nothing short of a frontal attack from the outside (i.e., a hostile takeover) or bankruptcy can dislodge them and clear the path for change. Again, this kind of situation is not uncommon, and the warning signs are easy to spot: inexistent, or ineffective boards of directors; passive outside shareholders (traders and sleepers); and inadequate executive succession planning.[5] Characteristically, the institutions of corporate governance come together in one person or economic actor and are strongly interrelated, making change in one impossible without changing all of the others.

II. Powers in a stalemate and change

The opposite of concentrated power over decision-making, namely powers in a stalemate, can also be the reason for change to be blocked. A clarification is perhaps in order at this point: when we speak of powers in a stalemate in the context of blocking change, we are not speaking of the general case of the publicly quoted firm in which shareholders are so widely dispersed that no single one of them is large enough to weigh in on decisions. In this context, management typically can and does make decisions that lead to a change in strategy, and, in some cases, in ownership (as described in Chapters 5). Rather, powers in a stalemate refers to two very specific constellations: (1) when opposing powers of decision-making effectively cancel each other out; and (2) when there are so many parties to consider in making decisions that nobody is able to take the lead.

Stalemate can occur between the management and elements of the ownership, within the management, or within the ownership. It arises from a balance of forces in which no one party to decision-making has the force (information, incentives, votes) to dominate the other. The most commonly evoked conflict pits management against ownership (the focus of agency theory), but in fact this does not very often end in stalemate. As described in Chapter 1, one or the other gains the upper hand and keeps it for the length of their involvement with the firm: management over traders and sleepers, or entrepreneurs (and/or activists) over management. Stalemate within management happens more frequently, particularly in large firms with complex, geographically dispersed operations. At Philips, for example, it took almost twenty years of declining performance (for most of the 1970s and all of the 1980s) until Jan Timmer (CEO, from 1990 to 1996) could begin to break up the stalemate within management (headquarters versus country managers) that had prevented the firm from rationalizing its international operations.[6]

In family firms and partnerships, and, under special circumstances also in publicly listed firms, stalemate within the ownership group can be a formidable obstacle to change. When different members of the family with roughly equal influence (and equivalent voting rights) disagree about the future of the firm, or when different partners are not of the same opinion, ownership, management, and strategy can persist for a long time, even in the face of poor performance. It is precisely to prevent this kind of stalemate that many family firms in the second or third generation initiate buyout schemes and go back to single-person ownership.[7] Partnerships may also try to buy out recalcitrant partners, or, as we saw in the case of Lazard Frères discussed in Chapter 1, bring in new partners from the outside to tip the balance and swing the vote. In the publicly listed firm, different shareholder groups can be at odds, and, if these groups are important and have roughly equal shareholdings, this can also lead to stalemate. This is the case at German travel concern TUI, already described in Chapter 1: with activists opposed to management and arguing for a change in corporate strategy on the one side and sleepers turned entrepreneurs on the other supporting the incumbent CEO, the firm is practically paralyzed, unwilling to make the changes demanded by the active investors, but unable to do much of anything else but maintain the status quo.

When a multitude of parties representing different types of interests are involved, decision-making change is not blocked as it is in a stalemate between opposing interests, but it can get so bogged down that no decisions are taken for a very long time. In the typical case, shareholder groups, stakeholder groups, and even management groups can find no common denominator upon which to base a plan for change. Japanese automaker Nissan lived through seven consecutive loss-making years in the 1990s and flirted with bankruptcy, while banks (as shareholders and creditors), unions, suppliers, and managers could not agree on what major changes needed to be made.[8] Almost the same story unfolded at Japan Air Lines (JAL) during the following decade, with the additional complication of government involvement. At Nissan, the 1999 equity alliance with Renault finally brought the strong ownership voice and the management decisiveness that was needed to change the corporate and business strategies of the firm. At JAL, bankruptcy and a restart under a new, government-supported ownership regime proved to be the only way to get the firm moving again.[9]

III. Separating powers and breaking up stalemates

In the publicly listed firm

A concentration of power and a stalemate of powers can have similar consequences. In both cases, the firm typically does not adequately address mistakes or shortcomings; and in both cases, change is very difficult. Ownership, management, and strategy are effectively tied in knots, and the only way to make change happen is to undo these knots. For change to occur in ownership, management, or strategy, somebody has to take the lead in breaking up the established balance of power. Poor economic performance, of its own, is not enough to motivate change in the kinds of power scenarios we have described in this chapter. Neither can traditional change management do the job. The most well-known frameworks of change management are focused on the internal organization and patently ignore questions of ownership and corporate governance.[10] The managers of Samsung reorganized the company during Chairman Lee's absence, to no measurable effect; the managers of Nissan tried practically every change management technique in the book, without success. For change management to work in the contexts described in this chapter, it is absolutely critical to address the underlying power issues.

> ### Point to watch: change management outside-in
>
> There are almost as many books about change management as there are about leadership. Even more so than the literature on strategy, the literature on change management focuses on managers as the agents of change. This manager-centric approach has two major drawbacks: first, it puts too much of a burden on managers to drive change; second, and more importantly, it distracts attention from the fact that, in many cases, change in the firm necessitates broader changes in ownership and governance. If shareholders and board members can block change, they can also enable change, and, in firms where change has been blocked for a long time, building a coalition of shareholders and board members can be a very good starting point for effecting a real transformation.

In the publicly listed firm, shareholders have the potential to change the existing balance of power by actively intervening: exerting pressure to dislodge management, if management has concentrated too much power upon itself; working to remove board members that contribute to maintaining an impasse; or aligning with other shareholders to break up a stalemate in ownership. Of course, neither the typical retail shareholder, not the typical institutional shareholder is likely to intervene in this manner. This is where the activists first described in Chapter 1 come into play, bringing a new perspective and, even more importantly, the ability to shake up the status quo. In some cases, activists may seek out the kind of situation we have described here as an opportunity, in order to profit from an uptick in the share price once other market participants recognize that a firm that has been locked into stalemate in its decision-making for a long time has a chance to change. In other cases, existing shareholders who are dissatisfied with how a firm has developed may approach activists with a view to getting them involved and tipping the balance of power toward change.

If we take the example of the Hermes UK Focus Funds (hereafter the "Focus Funds"), one of the most renowned and well-established activists, we see that the concept we have described as "addressing the underlying power issues" is not at all foreign to the actual practice of achieving change in situations where power, either concentrated or in a stalemate, is the primary cause for deadlock. The case of Tomkins plc, a British conglomerate that had delivered unsatisfactory results for a number of years and was run by a chairman cum CEO, Greg Hutchings, who had led the firm to great success in the 1980s and had a firm hold on decision-making (concentration of power), illustrates this very well.[11] The Focus Funds were initially contacted in 1999 by a group of dissatisfied shareholders who wanted the Focus Funds to join forces with them, call an extraordinary general meeting, and push Tomkins to reduce the scope of the firm (divest unrelated businesses). Rather than following this invitation and immediately risk a direct confrontation with management and the board, however, the Focus Funds decided first to talk to Hutchings and then contacted independent members of the board and other nondissident shareholders, in order to ascertain the general level of dissatisfaction with the CEO and the strategy and the potential for gaining allies in any fight to change the firm. Only once it became clear that Hutchings would not decisively lead change of his own accord and that there were enough stakeholders around who would side with them, did the Focus Funds join forces with the original group of dissatisfied shareholders and begin to openly campaign for major change. In the event, once he could see that the balance of power had shifted against him, Hutchings stepped back from the dual appointment and acquiesced to several major divestments and new board nominations that prepared the firm for a new beginning.

When shareholders are hopelessly deadlocked (situation of powers in a stalemate), it is also possible for *management* to take the initiative in addressing the underlying power issues. This is what happened in the case of Nissan in the late 1990s, where CEO Hanawa recognized that the firm could not change on its own (every possible internal change had been tried and failed) and needed help from the outside to overcome the stalemate between shareholders, creditors, and various other parties such as suppliers. In working through the implications of strategic alliances with DaimlerChrysler, Renault, and even Ford, Hanawa was able to put the debate about Nissan's future on a new factual basis and give the different stakeholders a set of pragmatic options to consider.[12] The equity alliance with Renault and the work put in by specialists from both sides eventually led to the successful turnaround of Nissan, but Hanawa's move to seriously consider alliances is what first gave Nissan a real chance for change.

Of course, nonshareholder managers take a big personal risk if they venture to address questions that are fundamentally part of ownership's domain. If nonshareholder managers do not play their cards right in this situation, they may lose their positions of influence and even their jobs. Nonshareholder managers need to be politically savvy and tread carefully. However, the key to management intervention in questions that touch upon the interests of stakeholders that are in a stalemate is information. If nonshareholder managers have superior information or, as in the case of Hanawa at Nissan, can gain access to superior information that changes the basis of debate among stakeholders and gives them concrete possibilities for action, then there is a chance that the stalemate and the vicious cycle of failure and inaction can be broken. In effect, information of this type can provide all or most of the stalemated stakeholders with a way out, and this is why it can be so powerful in unblocking the situation.[13]

In the privately held firm

How to deal with a concentration of power and its obverse, a stalemate of powers, in the privately held firm? Without the potential pressure from activists and a tightly limited circle of decision-makers, these questions seem even more intractable in the privately held firm. Traditionally in the case of the family firm, the board of directors, or in the absence of a board, a trusted advisor is called upon to speak to the founder who is unwilling to share their powers, or mediate among family members who are in a stalemate. This kind of interaction may help in getting people to talk to each other and in laying out the issues, but in our experience it rarely leads to softening stances. The difficulty of both the board and the trusted advisor is that they rarely have the capability to disrupt the existing constellation. As we have seen in the case of the publicly listed firm, the best way to break both concentration of power in an individual and power stalemates is to put forward a realistic alternative. Boards and advisors are often too close to the situation to be able to come up with such an alternative.

In the publicly listed firm, a realistic alternative to unlock a situation of power deadlock usually takes the shape of a new voice in ownership (i.e., an activist) or a new strategy. In the privately held firm, the entry of a new voice in ownership is often rejected out of hand. However, if the firm is in decline, even in slow decline, due to unresolved power issues, then the sale of a part or even all of the shares should be put on the agenda for consideration – not as a means of selling out, but rather as a way to get the firm moving again. The privately held firm has the luxury of choosing whom it will allow to enter into its shareholding structure. Building on the thinking developed in Chapter 1, it is sometimes possible to identify outsiders who will be interested in playing an active ownership role that both preserves the values the firm stands for and helps it overcome its power deadlock.[14]

A concrete new strategy can also contribute to getting the deadlocked private firm moving again. Depending on the context, there are many possible strategies to consider, and, here too, nonshareholder management can play an important role in bringing a viable alternative to the attention of the shareholders. Again, help is unlikely to come purely from the inside. If such an internal alternative were readily available, it would already have been put on the table. Perhaps even more than publicly listed firms that are continuously exposed to outside scrutiny and input, privately held firms that are by nature more inward looking need to look outside for a spark to unblock hardened ownership stances and strategy positions.[15] If the board of directors and/or trusted advisors to the privately held firm have the right external contacts and are willing to put them to use in this kind of situation, then these contacts should of course be fully explored. If not, then the firm and all of its stakeholders including nonshareholder management should think about how to get the right outsiders into the picture, to provide decision-makers with an actionable alternative to failure and continued inaction.

> **Point to watch: outside view in the privately held firm**
> Privately held firms like family firms and partnerships can become excessively focused on internal questions. This rarely happens

during the reign of the founder(s), but becomes more of an issue in the second and third generation. Because privately held firms tend to want to keep control over all of their operations, they are less likely than publicly held firms to explore partnerships with other firms. And yet, alliances and joint ventures provide one of the most powerful avenues for learning about how other firms do things, without the major financial risk associated with acquisitions. By engaging in a variety of business partnerships with other firms, privately held firms can avoid the tunnel vision that delegitimizes change and reinforces the status quo.

Despite failure, *no change in ownership, management, or strategy – conclusion*

It has to be acknowledged that both a concentration of power in an individual and a stalemate of powers are very difficult to overcome. We have encountered cases, both in the publicly listed and in the privately held spheres, in which the power deadlocks could not be broken. In these cases, decision-makers either underestimated the strength of the deadlock or did not come up with a viable alternative. Blinded by past success or survival against the odds, they may also have simply been too confident for too long and hence missed any opportunities to tip the balance of power in the firm towards real change. Of course, success or the illusion of success in the face of the signs of failure is also a persuasive inhibitor of change. In some firms, ownership, management, and strategy do not change, despite failure or because of the inability to admit failure; in others, success reinforces management, ownership, and strategy to the point of mutual rigidity.

SEVEN

Because of success, reinforcement of ownership, management, and strategy

Questions about ownership, management, and strategy tend to arise in the context of subpar performance or major change in the operating environment of the firm. When the firm is successful, especially if success has been durable, ownership, management, and strategy are much less likely to come under scrutiny. In fact, not a few observers seem to think that corporate governance, as a practical concern, only arises in the event of failure or wrongdoing.[1] Throughout this book, we have advocated a proactive approach to identifying and resolving issues that can significantly affect the well-being of the firm: not post hoc but ex ante. It is in this spirit that we now turn our attention to addressing the dangers of success. Just as the underlying causes of failure can go unnoticed or unacknowledged for a long time (as described in Chapter 6), the potential negative implications of success can also escape decision-makers for many years, until the erstwhile guarantors of success have turned into the sources of failure.[2]

Success has well-known risks, usually associated with the cognitive limitations of decision-makers and the inflexibility of organizations: overconfidence, failure to see the early signs of decline (myopia), and inertia.[3] From the point of view of the questions raised in this book, success is particularly interesting in cases where it prevents necessary and timely changes in ownership, management, and strategy, what we will term the *governance rigidity of success*. In our research, we identify two distinct sources of the governance rigidity of success: a particular person, either a manager or an owner; or a particular strategic formula for success. In the first case, success becomes identified with one person (or, less commonly, a small group of people), and no counterweight can emerge to challenge the vision articulated by that person. In the second case, people in the firm equate success with a particular strategic formula and are unable to respond to changes in the environment that can eventually invalidate that formula. In the most extreme cases of the governance rigidity of success, the person stands for the formula, and the formula is identified with the person. In the following, however, we will treat the two types separately.

I. Attribution of past success to a single individual

In both publicly listed and privately held firms, success can be attributed to and identified with an individual. In the publicly listed firm, this individual is usually a nonshareholder manager who has turned the fortunes of the firm around (like Carlos Ghosn at Nissan or Sergio Marchionne at Fiat) or has grown the firm beyond expectations (like Jamie Dimon at JP MorganChase); in the privately held firm, this is usually the founder, or, in rarer cases, a successor who has contributed decisively to the success of the firm. Since Steve Jobs actually combines all of these characteristics (founder, turnaround artist, and growth executive), Apple represents a particularly fascinating case for studying how a firm can address the threat of the governance rigidity of success. In effect, at Apple, ownership, management, and strategy are so closely tied to one person that it was very difficult for the firm to plan for succession.

Success attributed to an individual can be recognized by two principal outward signs: (a) the external perception and reputation of the firm is very closely tied to one person – shareholders, customers, and media regularly refer to the firm and the person in the same breath; (b) the internal discourse of the firm is also dominated by reference to the person – has x been informed? What does x think? What would x do? etc. In effect, both external stakeholders and internal staff identify the firm and its success with one special individual. Note that success attributed to an individual, as described here, is distinct from the sense of identification with leading executive and/or shareholder personalities that exists in some form in every organization. What we are talking about is an extreme variant of attribution that traces the success of a whole (large) firm almost entirely to the genius or skill of one individual.[4]

Over and above the risks of overconfidence and myopia that are present in every situation of sustained success, attributing the success of a firm to one individual also poses severe governance risks. First and most importantly, power over decision-making will tend to become narrowly concentrated in the person of the successful executive or owner. Formal checks on the person's power such as boards of directors with nonexecutive-led committees and decentralized organizational structures with management autonomy might be in place, but they do not function as meaningful constraints on the individual on whom the success of the firm supposedly depends. Whatever they says goes, and no opposing internal or external voice can get any traction. In the context of an all-powerful individual, the counterpoint of power, accountability, is also weakened. Not only does the individual have power to make decisions at will, they may also be able to avoid accountability when things do not go well – after all, everyone else (including the board) has also signed off on the decisions, so there is no one in the firm who can legitimately call the successful executive or shareholder to account.

Unlimited power and inadequate accountability disable the linkages between ownership, management, and strategy discussed in this book and make it as easy for the signs of failure to go unheeded as it is for success to perpetuate itself. Just like in the case of failure described in Chapter 6, outsiders and proposals from the outside play a critical role in unlocking the concentration of power in the case of success. However, a firm that is in the thrall of a successful executive or shareholder can be even more difficult to change than a firm that has a history of failure. Without tackling the corporate governance system and changing the balance of power, outsiders and insiders with "outside" ideas have very little chance of making their warnings heard ex ante, before the psychological phenomena of overconfidence and myopia lead the firm into dangerous waters. In effect, we can expect concentration of power based on success attribution to a single individual to be a very fertile context for falling into these well-known traps of success.

> #### Point to watch: all-powerful leaders
>
> Working with an all-powerful leader presents many challenges – for publicly listed firms as much as for private firms. The question of timing can be critical, as it is much easier to begin to address the issues raised here when a leader is still flexible enough to think about alternatives for the firm, as well as for himself or herself. Thus, a good rule of thumb for a family firm is to organize succession plans before the combined age of the patriarch and the person next in line exceeds a hundred years. More generally, board members and other members of the executive team need to be vigilant about the outward signs of a concentration of power around the successful leader and put in place institutional limitations before it becomes impossibly difficult to do so.

II. Attribution of past success to a strategic formula

Where the rigidity of success can be traced to the firm's adherence to a strategic formula, rather than a focus on a particular person, the formula itself is put on a pedestal where it cannot be criticized or even doubted. Thus, at investment banks such as

Bear Stearns and Lehman Brothers or at the investment banking divisions of commercial banks like UBS and RBS, the amazing apparent successes of the subprime mortgage trading desks did not face serious questioning from senior executives and boards.[5] Not everybody understood why or how a small group of people could generate such a disproportionate share of firm profits, but the formula appeared to work, and that was enough for decision-makers at many of these institutions. Of course, the fact that everyone in the industry was doing the same thing also helped reinforce the strategic formula for success in investment banking, but this is not a necessary prerequisite. Indeed, some firms will pursue their strategic formula precisely with the objective of preserving what makes them unique: for example, IBM's adherence to mainframe computers into the 1980s despite the emergence of the PC, Toys 'R' Us sticking with the toys superstore concept through the 1990s and into 2000 in the face of debilitating competition from discount retailers and online shopping, or Nokia's inability to transition from traditional mobile phones to smart phones in the 2000s.[6] In all of these cases of success turning into failure, the strength of the firm's strategic formula for success prevented constructive dialogue, both within management and between management and ownership. The strategic formula for success had become the sole point of reference for ownership, management, and strategy.

If it is as dominant as described here, a strategic formula for success also poses severe governance risks. Decision-making power in the firm is not balanced, but concentrated around the formula and the people who stand for the formula, and dissenters cannot get a proper hearing. If and when the formula is threatened or starts to lose validity, the firm will fail to react – not in the first instance because of organizational inertia, the organization's inability to change course, but because of the lack of effective governance associated with the rigidity of success. Consider the situation of Toyota up until 2010: absolute industry leadership in quality control, dominance in its key markets (Japan and the US), and years of seemingly unstoppable international growth. Under these circumstances, it is not surprising that the firm saw little need to adjust its institutions of governance beyond creating a star-studded, but relatively isolated international advisory board. In the event, no one was able to effectively question the strategy of unbridled international growth, and the concerned voices of factory engineers who worried about the maintenance of quality standards went unheeded. Even though the crisis of confidence turned out to be overblown and partially unfounded, the string of accidents and recalls that culminated in the Toyota chairman's public apology to the United States Congress in 2011 did a lot of damage to the reputation of the firm.[7] Adjustments in governance that made decision-makers more sensitive to the governance risks inherent in adhering to a strategic formula for success could have done a lot to prevent matters from escaping the control of the firm.

As in the case of success attributed to one person, the governance risks of a strategic formula for success are best addressed by guaranteeing that strong outsiders have a voice in decision-making. This may be at the level of the board of directors, if nonexecutives have sufficiently deep familiarity with the workings of the organization and are willing to play an active role in shaping strategic decisions. If this is not the case, then the firm needs to periodically refresh internal governance processes. This is best done by bringing in new people from time to time, rather than relying exclusively on adjustments to formal structures and procedures. Among shareholders, entrepreneurs should pay more attention to strategy, especially in cases where the strategic formula for success has remained unchanged for a long time. If the firm is publicly listed, activists may also play a role in the strategic debate, although they usually only buy in after things have started to go wrong. In sum, all stakeholders need to be proactive about questioning the strategic formula for success, particularly when it is deeply entrenched.

Point to watch: strategic formula in an age of personality

In an age in which individual personalities attain unprecedented fame in all walks of life, including business, a strategic formula is quite likely to be associated with a particular person. This can make it even more difficult for shareholders and executives who are not part of the leader's entourage to make themselves heard. By questioning the strategic formula, you are automatically also questioning the leader, and this is fraught with danger for the questioner. In this kind of situation, it is important to be able to propose concrete positive alternatives that can be set up as experiments, rather than to try to effect a major sea change in one go. The results of experiments with change can help build confidence in alternative paths.

Because of success, *reinforcement of ownership, management, and strategy – conclusion*

Sustained success implies governance risks. Particularly where success is attributed to one person or associated with a strategic formula, ownership, management, and strategy tend to reinforce each other around the person or the formula, necessary change is delayed or inhibited, and the governance risks are pronounced. Ensuring strong outside voices have an influence in decision-making is the best way to mitigate these risks.

PART III

Concluding remarks

In Part III we have shown that the relationship between ownership, management, and strategy is reciprocal – not only do changes in ownership and management affect strategy, but changes in strategy also shape the structure of ownership and the identity of management. We have argued that changes in strategy can redistribute power among shareholders and among managers, as well as between the two groups of actors. The choice of a particular corporate strategy and of specific business strategies plays into the hands of some and goes against the wishes of others. Those who find their positions reinforced by the choice of strategy will assume an even bigger role in decision-making going forward, while those who are weakened by the choice of strategy may be relegated to the sidelines or leave the firm altogether. Thus, we can say that the choice of strategy represents both the outcome of a political confrontation and the basis for future political confrontations among shareholders and managers over the future of the firm.

The observation that failure and success in the marketplace do not necessarily lead to adaptation in the expected direction, but can rather reinforce existing positions and prevent change, makes it all the more important for all stakeholders to recognize and work with the power constellation in the firm as it is, not as it should be in an idealized world of purely rational economic considerations. Strategy is for the firm, but strategy decisions are taken in light of the different values, the different methods, and the substitutability of shareholders and managers. If we want to reconcile the practice of strategy with the reality of shareholders and managers, we cannot avoid the question of "cui bono" – strategy for whom?

Background reading – Part III

Bartlett, C., Ghoshal, S., and Birkinshaw, J. *Transnational Management* (third edn.), New York: MacMillan, 2003.

Beer, M. and Noria, N. *Breaking the Code of Change*, Cambridge, MA: Harvard Business School Press, 2000.

Cyert, R. M. and March, J. G. *A Behavioral Theory of the Firm*, New Jersey: Prentice-Hall, 1963.

Fredrickson, J. (ed.) *Perspectives on Strategic Management*, New York: HarperCollins, 1990.

Galbraith, J. R. and Kazanjian, R. K. *Strategy Implementation: Structure, Systems, and Process* (second edn.), St. Paul, MN: West, 1986.

Grant, R. M. *Contemporary Strategy Analysis* (seventh edn.), New York: Wiley, 2009.

Kotter, J. P. *Leading Change*, Cambridge, MA: Harvard Business School Press, 1996.

Liker, J. K. and Ogden, T. N. *Toyota Under Fire*, New York: McGraw-Hill, 2011.

March, J. G. and Simon, H. A. *Organizations*, New York: Wiley, 1958.

Miller, D. and Friesen, P. *Organizations: A Quantum View*, Englewood Cliffs, NJ: Prentice-Hall, 1984.

Nee, V. and Swedberg, R. (eds.) *The Economic Sociology of Capitalism*, Princeton University Press, 2005.

Nonaka, I. and Takeuchi, H. *The Knowledge-creating Company: How Japanese Companies Create the Dynamics of Innovation*, Oxford University Press, 1995.

Rumelt, R. P. *Strategy, Structure, and Economic Performance*, Boston: Division of Research, Graduate School of Business Administration, Harvard University, 1974.

Szulanski, G., Doz, Y., and Porac, J. (eds.) *Advances In Strategic Management* (Vol. XXII), Bingley, UK: Emerald Group Publishing Limited, 2006.

Useem, M. *Investor Capitalism: How Money Managers Are Changing the Face of Corporate America*, New York: Basic Books, 1996.

PART IV

Implications for corporate governance

We have painted an explicitly political picture of the corporation, one in which the principal actors, shareholders and managers, negotiate over strategy against the background of their own particular values and methods, as well as their substitutability. Such a political or even politicized view of the corporation naturally has significant implications for corporate governance, as it pertains directly to the question of who is in charge. Along the way, we have pointed out how changes in ownership, management, and strategy can put strains on the systems of corporate governance in place: changes in ownership, by changing the balance of power among different types of shareholders, may render existing understandings about the direction of the firm immaterial; changes in management may lead to long-term shifts in how the firm is run; and changes in strategy can trigger risks that the firm's governance infrastructure cannot adequately capture or address. In this concluding section, we will elaborate on the implications of our perspective for the institutions of corporate governance, with a special focus on the board of directors (Chapter 8), and the different interests behind strategic decision-making (Conclusion).

EIGHT

The board of directors

"Corporate governance and strategy" is the subtitle of this book, but the first seven chapters do not contain a single section dedicated to the institution of the board of directors. This is not because we think the board is unimportant in the corporate governance of the firm. Our view is that the board of directors cannot be understood as an independent body, without reference to shareholders and managers. This is why we did not tackle the question of the board until the different characteristics of shareholders and managers and the critical aspects of corporate and business strategy – in failure and in success – had been described and discussed.

As an institution, the board of directors has in recent years been both reified and vilified. On the one hand, the board, and, in particular, the positions of chairperson and independent director have been at the heart of efforts to improve corporate governance. Since the 1992 Cadbury Report, if not earlier, reformers have stressed the importance of independence on the board and put much of their hope for better corporate governance on boards taking a more active role in shaping strategy and monitoring management.[1] At the same time, the actual performance of the board of directors has been continuously criticized. The full-page picture advertisement of a silhouette of the board of directors of Sears Roebuck, with the tagline the "non-performing assets of Sears," taken out in the *Wall Street Journal* in April 1992 by activist investor Robert Monks, is symptomatic of this attitude, widespread among shareholders and the general public.[2] What is the real status of the board – supreme body of the corporation with ultimate responsibility or mere decoration, with little to say to managers or shareholders?

The purpose and the role of the board of directors differ according to the jurisdiction.[3] From the point of view of the arguments about shareholders, managers, and strategy advanced in this book, the most relevant formal distinction concerns the ultimate purpose of the board of directors. Whom should the board of directors serve and what should it try to achieve? In most jurisdictions, including the United Kingdom, Germany, France, and Japan, the board of directors is supposed to serve the interests of the corporation, maintaining its long-term viability. Thus, in the United Kingdom, for example, the board of directors "should lead and control the company, [being] collectively responsible for success; all directors must take decisions objectively *in the interests of the company*" (emphasis added). In other words, the UK board (like the German or the French) is supposed to be a neutral body with a fiduciary duty towards the corporation as a whole, without preference for one group of stakeholders over another.[4] For historical reasons connected to the stock market crash of 1929 and the ensuing regulation of the exchanges by the SEC (Securities and Exchange Commission),[5] the United States has evolved towards a different model, one in which the board of directors has "the important role of overseeing management performance *on behalf of stockholders*; [its] primary duties are to select and oversee management and monitor its performance and adherence to corporate standards" (emphasis added). In practice this means that the American board of directors is not neutral, but rather places the interests of shareholders above the interests of other stakeholders. In line with agency theory thinking, the American board is supposed to protect shareholders from the possible missteps of management. And yet, the fact that the American board of directors should look out indiscriminately for the interests of *all* shareholders also makes it apolitical. Like its counterparts in Europe and elsewhere, the American board of directors has a fiduciary duty to uphold the general good.

In view of the board of directors' fiduciary duty toward the general good, it makes sense that recent efforts to reform corporate governance have focused on ensuring the independence of the board as a decision-making body. With an independent chairperson and (in many jurisdictions) a majority of independent directors, the board should, in theory at least, not be beholden to any particular interests. Of course, governance codes and regulations do not and cannot define what constitutes the interests of the corporation or the interests of the shareholders in the general case. This is left up to the board of directors who have to deal with the reality of diverging interests, both between shareholders and managers and within these groups, as described in this book. Despite being subject to election and replacement by the shareholders and being obliged to get much of the information they need to make decisions from the managers, directors are called upon to be neutral and ignore the particular interests of shareholders and managers. This is a very difficult position to uphold, and, in practice, directors are often co-opted by one subgroup or another, resulting in shareholder-dominated boards or management-dominated boards.[6] How can the neutrality of the board be reconciled with the intensely political nature of the struggle among shareholders and managers for influence over strategy?

Point to watch: neutrality of the board

Board members cannot be compared to judges and should not be held to the same standards of impartiality. Unlike judges, board members do not have a code or a body of law to refer to as the supreme authority governing their decisions, but must rely on their own assessments of what constitutes the appropriate way forward for the firm. However, they should not be beholden to any particular party in a way that clouds their judgment. In theory, independent directors are not obligated to anybody but the firm, but independence alone does not guarantee that directors actually exercise judgment in a considered and conscientious manner.

In the following we will make the argument that the board of directors, while remaining neutral in its duty to uphold the general good of the corporation, needs to take the different values and methods, as well as the substitutability of both shareholders and managers into account in its decision-making. As we have shown in the preceding chapters, particular interests cannot be avoided in the business firm. It is one thing to structure the board so as to preclude any particular interests from dominating the agenda ex ante, it is quite another to argue that the board should not pay attention to particular interests. Boards of directors need to address the reality of particular interests in weighing the pros and cons of their decisions, or else they risk being relegated to irrelevance, as shareholders and managers try to shape strategy to suit their own interests.

I. In search of the ideal board of directors

A great deal of research has gone into attempting to define the structural characteristics of the ideal board of directors.[7] On this basis, prescriptions have been made for composition, size, and term of office, but also for structuring (i.e., committees) and meeting procedure. In all of this work, two points stand out: first, the emphasis on building independence into the structure of boards and, second, the insignificant relationships generally reported between the structure of the board and the performance of the firm. Indeed, while independence (i.e., of individual directors, of the chairperson, of the committees) does not appear to hurt performance, it also does not seem to add much.[8]

Apart from the statistical difficulty of demonstrating the link between variables that are separated by so many intermediate variables, there are also conceptual difficulties arising from the equivocal qualities of independence. While independence of the board of directors ought to promote long-term thinking, unbiased judgment, and the pursuit of carefully constructed strategies in line with the board's fiduciary duties, in practice independence can also be associated with a lack of commitment on the part of board members. If only weakly committed, independents are easy to sway, and co-optation by different shareholder or manager groupings can become a severe problem – some boards may be independent only in name.

Although the recent focus on independence has made boards more cognizant of and responsive to their fiduciary duties, there have been many cases of corporate governance failure over the last decade in which the negatives of independence have turned out to be more real than the positives.[9] From Enron to WorldCom, and from Citibank to UBS, boards of directors met the most up to date criteria for independence and accordingly received high marks from the providers of corporate governance ratings. Research conducted subsequent to the unraveling of these firms and/or their strategies revealed that independent directors had not been able to prevent disaster: too superficial in their involvement, too close to management in their outlook, or too weak.

As depicted in Table 8.1 below, in situations where either manager power or shareholder power is high, a board that is composed primarily of independents typically serves as a rubber stamp for the party in power. In the uncommon case where manager power and shareholder power are both low, the board has the potential to effectively become a third power, stepping into the vacuum left by indecisive managers and divided shareholders. The role of the board

TABLE 8.1 *The role of the board as a reflection of the power of managers and shareholders*

		Power of shareholders	
		High	Low
Power of managers	High	Board as arbiter	Manager control
	Low	Shareholder control	Board as third power

takes on all its significance when both managers and shareholders are powerful and disagree over strategy: this is when a knowledgeable, experienced, and committed board can act as an arbiter and prevent the debilitating stalemates described in Chapter 6. The problem is that the prevailing focus on independence does not in any way guarantee that the board of directors will have the strength to take on this critical role.

Are we therefore to conclude that the focus on independence has been misplaced and that the board of directors, as it is currently structured, is ultimately condemned to irrelevance? Certainly, it is becoming increasingly difficult to uphold the conception of an apolitical institution in a fundamentally political environment. The practice of ignoring differences between and among shareholders and managers does not appear to further the general good. Independence is also poorly suited to the governance of the modern business firm, if it implies a lack of commitment and leads to superficial judgment. In an ever more complex world, the board needs to have deep knowledge of both the firm and its context. Finally, a board of directors composed principally of outsiders meeting only at fixed intervals is likely to have trouble keeping up with market and technology developments when conditions are volatile.

Recognizing the limitations of the board of directors as currently constituted, shareholder activists such as the Hermes Pensions Management and Governance for Owners (both of the United

Kingdom) have argued for quite some time that shareholders should play a larger role in both direction and oversight.[10] Although this suggestion has the merit of rendering the political nature of strategic decision-making explicit and puts the onus on shareholders to tend to their interests,[11] it is not clear how shareholders who have multiple holdings to oversee and are not privy to any special information from management can overcome the problems of superficiality and timeliness. Indeed, even the best-informed and most dedicated shareholders are likely to be further away from the reality of the firm than the board of directors.

Point to watch: shareholders as board members

In publicly listed firms, traders and activists rarely seek to become board members: being on the board would make them privy to inside information and prevent them from freely selling their shares. Entrepreneurs and sleepers are much more likely to join the boards of the firm(s) they own shares in, with the explicit objective of protecting their interests. Shareholders who are also board members wear multiple hats and have to recognize that they also have a fiduciary responsibility towards shareholders who are not represented on the board. In practice, shareholder board members can be a powerful force for maintaining a long-term perspective.

II. From independence to relevance: transforming the board of directors

The attempt to create an institutional structure that is independent of the different interests of shareholders and managers and ignores how their value, method, and substitutability influence the choice of strategy has not measurably improved corporate governance. If, as the preceding chapters have shown, differences between and among shareholders and managers are critical to shaping the direction of the firm, then the board of directors needs to consider these explicitly. We do not wish to argue for corporate governance by numerical representation[12] – strict adherence to representation runs counter to the valid principle of independence and can lead to the neglect of minority rights.[13] Rather, we propose that the board should be the place where disagreements between shareholders and managers (as well as among managers and among shareholders) are openly discussed and where a dominant coalition is allowed to emerge. This idea is graphically expressed in Figure 8.1 below.

Efforts to reform corporate governance that have focused on the structure of the board of directors in general and the independence of directors in particular have not been misguided, but they are incomplete. Sufficiently committed and appropriately involved, independent directors who have the general good at heart can still be a great force for effective governance in the firm. As we have pointed out, however, independence alone is not enough and may give stakeholders in the firm an unfounded sense of security. To get to the bottom of what is driving the interests of shareholders and managers and weigh them against their own views on what is right, independent directors need to be much more deeply implicated, spending more time on the job of being a member of the board and developing their own sense of the firm's strengths and weaknesses. It is this kind of reasoning that leads Hilti to require of its independent directors a minimum time commitment of twenty days a year

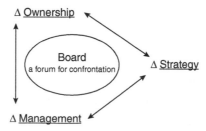

Figure 8.1 Shareholders, management, and strategy: the role of the board.

and participation in one major corporate project, in addition to the duties generally associated with a board of directors.[14] Only when they are thus committed and integrated, can independent directors meaningfully stand up for the general good that they are supposed to defend.

> **Point to watch: commitment of the board**
>
> Many boards and many board members are unwilling to stand up for what they believe to be the right course of action, preferring to "make a note of it in the minutes" or to avoid conflict altogether. True commitment cannot be bought with money or forced with the threat of legal action; it arises from deep involvement with the firm – time spent, decisions taken, and projects seen through. If boards are to serve as a locus of confrontation over the future of the firm and to integrate different points of view, then board members have to be ready to put together their own arguments and be willing to personally deal with all of the relevant players.

The emphasis on independent directors assumes that a neutral "best" strategy can be found, independent of the interests of particular shareholders and managers; if strategy is, in fact, driven by different interests, as we have argued, then the board ought to function as a transparent forum for addressing these perspectives. This means that board processes have to be adapted to give time for consideration of shareholders' and managers' points of view, and directors, both independent and otherwise, have to make time for drawing the different strands together. Taking this line of reflection to its logical conclusion suggests that boards of directors become more proactive in the decision-making processes of strategy and governance. Only by becoming more proactive can the board make sure that subgroups of shareholders and/or managers do not take strategy into their own hands.

The board of directors – conclusion

However committed and involved, the board of directors is just one element of the corporate governance system of the firm. In general, a corporate governance system should protect the firm from one or another interest group "hijacking" the firm for its own purposes. This is why it is important to ensure that not only the board of directors, but also the information and control structures of the firm are set up in such a manner that the potential conflicts of shareholder and manager interests are given adequate consideration. In practice, this means that changes in ownership, management, and strategy require adaptation of the governance systems in place. Thus, an IPO that brings in new, substitutable shareholders with different values and methods should be accompanied by the introduction of mechanisms to track the identities of these shareholders (see Chapter 3); similarly, the appointment of a new CEO with a track record of radical change is the right occasion to rethink how the performance of management is measured and rewarded (see Chapter 2); a major change in corporate or business strategy, finally, necessitates a new assessment of risk and the monitoring of risk (see Chapter 5). Throughout the book, we have argued that the sophistication of the corporate governance system in place needs to reflect the complexity of the interactions among shareholders and managers and the difficulty of the strategy. The more diverse the different relationships and the more challenging the strategy, the better the system has to be. With a change in ownership, management, *or* strategy, the firm is exposed to strains that test the adequacy of both the board of directors and the information and control structures that constitute its corporate governance system.

The ultimate objective of corporate governance systems is to ensure the continuity of the firm.[15] Changes in ownership, management, and strategy can threaten the continuity of the firm, if not properly governed. By conceiving of corporate governance in terms of the means rather than the end, many commentators obscure the ultimate objective of corporate governance. The means – corporate constitutions, boards of directors, information and control structures, and so forth – cannot be defined once and for all. Rather, the means of corporate governance need to be adapted with changes in ownership, management, and strategy, to make sure that the end of corporate governance can still be achieved. The political landscape of many firms is very dynamic, with multiple and changing actors interacting to try to shape strategy to suit their own interests. Corporate governance systems need to be reviewed and modified accordingly.

Conclusion – strategy for whom?

In opening the black box of agency theory to consider how shareholders and managers differ among themselves, and in exploring how decisions are made when these actors come to different conclusions about the direction of the firm, we have presented a political picture of strategy. In our view, strategic choices are the outcome of a political process and, in turn, create a new political reality, strengthening some, weakening others, and, if the firm's ownership and management structures are open, in due course attracting new shareholders and new managers. Such a political picture of strategy would appear to go against the received wisdom of strategy as rational choice: if strategy is the outcome of a political process, then it might be the preferred solution only for a particular group.[1] Some shareholders and managers will benefit, while others may be poorly served or less well off.

For scholars of strategic management as well as for business schools and MBAs, the conclusion that strategic choices obey the logic of particular interests, benefitting different shareholders and different managers unequally, is deeply troubling. If strategy, and by extension, the board of directors, do not always promote the general good, then every strategic decision needs to be reviewed in terms of the question "cui bono." This means that the idea of one best strategy cannot always be upheld. Strategists and managers have to take the views of different shareholders into account, while shareholders have to think about the perspectives of different managers. In general, stakeholders have to consider the values and methods of the actors involved and recognize the relevance of their substitutability in evaluating the outlook of the firm.

I. What is good for the firm and who decides?

What is good for the firm in the long run may not be good for some shareholders and managers, while what is good for some shareholders and managers may not be good for the firm. It is one thing to acknowledge that this state of affairs can exist in practice, it is quite another to make it a basis for analyzing how firms evolve.

The French government report (*rapport Sartorius*) and the ensuing public discussion of the strategic choices made by ailing automobile manufacturer PSA (Peugeot/Citroen) provide a fascinating case in point.[2] In brief, the Sartorius report criticizes PSA for having failed to internationalize early enough and for having been slow to build cross-border partnerships, while at the same time paying (relatively) generous dividends and repurchasing shares. The report links this failure to invest in an international future with the founding Peugeot family's purported desire to maintain control and to benefit financially. In other words, the Peugeot family, owning 25 percent of the shares and controlling 38 percent of the voting rights, is supposed to have influenced the strategy of the firm to further its own agenda, against the interests of other shareholders and stakeholders such as managers and employees, many of whom now stand to lose their jobs as the firm closes French factories and retrenches.

The analysis contained in the Sartorius report makes explicit reference to the political nature of strategic decision-making, but is it really a question of PSA having picked the "wrong" strategy to benefit the particular interests of the family? In France, the comparison is often made between PSA and Renault. Today (2013), Paris-based Renault appears to be doing much better than its longtime rival from the Alsace: with a market capitalization more than three times higher, with (moderate) profits rather than losses, and with a better market position, Renault looks like a relative success, given the comparable starting points of the two firms in the late 1990s. Clearly, Renault internationalized earlier and more deeply than Peugeot, both in terms of equity partnerships (principally with Nissan, as discussed in Chapter 5, but also with the Russian AvtoVAZ and the German Daimler) and in terms of production and sales (Renault is less Europe focused, with strong positions in emerging markets). While ostensibly diluting the control the firm has over its own fortunes, the equity partnerships have allowed Renault to tap new skills and new markets and paid handsome financial dividends. PSA, as we have seen, was late to develop major partnerships and has remained much more deeply anchored in France. Operating in the same industry and faced with the same pressures arising from globalization, the two firms made very different strategic choices, and their relative positions appear to show Renault as the clear winner.

Given the gulf separating the performance of the two firms today, it is easy to forget that Renault's strategy was not always universally acclaimed. In fact, when the strategic alliance with Nissan was first announced, in March of 1999, the share price of Renault began a steep decline, amid worries that Renault would never make a go of its plans to first revive Nissan and then benefit from sharing engineering and production skills with its Japanese partner. Even after Nissan had been turned around (2001), Renault had difficulty in convincing the financial markets to buy into its bi-national approach: for quite some time, the market capitalization of Renault was approximately equivalent to the firm's 44 percent stake in Nissan, meaning that the assets of Renault were effectively valued at zero. Despite the firm's relative success in the marketplace, some activist shareholders criticized Renault for its corporate governance, taking issue with the cross-holding structure in which Renault owns 44 percent of Nissan and Nissan owns 15 percent of Renault. By contrast, during the early years of the first decade of the twenty-first century, PSA was being praised for staying the course and not engaging in international adventures. The firm seemed to have found a way to grow organically and survive without outside support.

The comparison between PSA and Renault illustrates two of the key points we have articulated in this book. First, there can be significant disagreement about what constitutes the "right" strategy (and the "correct" governance structure), between shareholders and managers, as described by agency theory, but also among shareholders and among managers. For their own reasons, different shareholder groups continued to criticize the strategy of Renault and some sold off their shares, even after that strategy had begun to pay off in competitive and financial terms. At PSA, starting in 2007, a succession of two new CEOs hired from outside the firm and outside the industry tried, but could not achieve a change in course. Second, and more fundamental to the argument, where there is disagreement over strategy, there will also be a political conflict over strategy, with a dominant coalition that eventually imposes its views, based on its own values and methods, and in light of its own substitutability. At Renault, the French state, the largest shareholder at the time of the decision to partner with Nissan (46 percent), went along with management's proposal to internationalize the firm, in full awareness of the possibility that its stake and its influence would be diluted; at PSA, the Peugeot family apparently weighed in against such a move for a very long time (until 2012, when an agreement was signed with GM, giving the American firm a 7 percent stake in PSA). In order to understand the strategic choices of firms, in other words, it is necessary to understand what drives the formation and evolution of dominant coalitions between and among shareholders and managers.

Strategic choice and the dominant coalition

If enough time has elapsed since the time of a decision, it is easy to see what would have been the right strategic choice. Today, Renault looks like it made the smarter decision than Peugeot, but we say this with the wisdom of hindsight. Whether a strategic choice turns out be right depends on how the context evolves and how the firm adapts. In most cases, there are alternatives to be considered, and none of the approaches on the table can possibly deal with all unforeseen circumstances. In other words, although there may be strategies that are clearly wrong for the firm and the context, there is not a unique "good strategy" out there, waiting to be discovered.[3] Instead, there are different strategies to be considered, some better suited to the environment and the skill base of the firm than others, perhaps, but none with a monopoly on economic rationality, given that the future is always uncertain. Where there is a real choice to be made, the question of "who decides" becomes critical. Different stakeholders – shareholders, managers, and members of the board – may have different views of what constitutes the right way forward for a firm. These differences will be justified in economic terms, but, as we have shown, they are not merely differences of rational assessment. They are also symptomatic of the fact that different actors want different things out of their association with the firm. The analysis presented in this book provides a framework for understanding how these different perspectives on strategy can arise, based on the characteristics of the actors and on their positions in the structure of the firm. If we were to sum up the argument in light of the cases of Renault and Peugeot, we would say that the dominant coalition of shareholders and managers at Renault, in line with their own interests, made the problematical choice to internationalize, while the dominant coalition of shareholders and managers at Peugeot, in line with *their* own interests, made the equally difficult choice to stay put. Both were legitimate choices, when viewed against the characteristics and positions of the main actors and the constellation of power in the respective firms.

Point to watch: conservatism can be better

The international expansion strategy of Soufflet SA, the French family firm that has risen to the number two position worldwide in the malt industry contrasts with the stories of Renault and PSA and nicely illustrates the statement that there is no one right strategy. Whereas its publicly listed competitors were quick to invest in new sources of barley in Latin America and China when the demand for beer boomed in the early 2000s, Soufflet did not want to borrow or open up its capital and initially stayed on the sidelines. While the other firms were discovering that their new sources did not have the quality necessary to produce consistently for the beer industry (the principal market for malt), Soufflet was quietly buying up Eastern European sources of barley, benefitting from the aid of the European Union and a few well-chosen partnerships (i.e., in Russia) to surpass every one of its competitors but the largest, while still maintaining full family ownership. In other words, where PSA's conservatism eventually worked to its disadvantage, Soufflet's conservatism turned out to be the best way forward, given the desire of the decision-makers to maintain the governance model of the firm. With the perspective of ten years, it is possible to say that Soufflet made the right decision.

Differences over strategy are usually couched in terms of different assumptions about markets and resources. Our analysis suggests the need to go beyond a discussion of economic assumptions in interpreting the strategic choices of firms. Conceiving of strategic decision-making as a political process involving multiple actors with different interests, including governance interests, we find that the reasoning behind strategic choices can be better understood if we take the values, methods, and substitutability of decision-makers into consideration. Shareholders and managers alike can influence strategy, and it is not a matter of indifference to the fortunes of the firm if activists (see Chapter 1 on changes in ownership) are pushing for a breakup, or if adopters are campaigning for the latest fashions (see Chapter 2 on changes in management). In thinking about how changes in ownership and management affect the choice of strategy one can obtain a more accurate picture of where the firm is headed, if one focuses not only on what the different shareholders and managers want for the firm, but also what they want for themselves and how they are positioned to achieve their objectives. Strategy is intended for the benefit of the firm, but it can also be used to the advantage of some shareholders and managers, and against others.

Our perspective helps explain why firms go through distinctive phases in their strategic evolution, phases that can turn into eras, if the dominant coalition of shareholders and managers is durable enough. As long as key shareholders and key managers maintain their power over other shareholders and other managers and continue to agree among themselves, the same mix of values, methods, and substitutability will exercise controlling influence over the choice of strategy. Recall the case of TUI described in detail in Chapter 1: ever since first taking over in 1996, CEO Michael Frenzel has managed to line up enough shareholder support to allow him to continue to lead the firm on a path of poorly timed diversification in cyclical industries, fighting off the strategy recommendations of large activist shareholders, in spite of many years of mediocre performance. Eventually, we would expect Frenzel's coalition to be ousted from power, but as long as it is not, the firm's strategy will faithfully reflect the desires of the CEO. More generally, dominant coalitions come and go, and strategies come and go. Often, but not always (see Chapter 6), poor performance is enough to dislodge the people who are directing the firm. In other cases, it is the change of generations (i.e., of family members, or of executives) that brings a new dominant coalition to the fore and brings about a change in strategy. Of course, phases in the strategic evolution of firms always occur against the background of shifting economic realities, and we would not wish to ignore these in our analysis. What this book highlights is the power of dominant coalitions in explaining periods of strategic stability and instances of strategic change, sometimes in line with the economic context of the firm, but at other times in opposition to economic rationale and in support of particularistic interests.

Point to watch: eras of leadership

Eras of leadership do not necessarily match economic or competitive cycles. In fact, more likely than not, there will be a mismatch between the two. As a political construct, an era of leadership depends on the confluence of interests of multiple players and can be very hard to dislodge. Thus, changing the CEO in reaction to changing economic realities may or may not lead to a fundamental reassessment of strategy. Similarly, declaring a change in the strategy is often insufficient to effect real change, because the players who are really in charge, namely key shareholders and key managers, remain the same. Leadership can be a lot stickier than business, and therefore firms are often slow to adapt their governance to changed realities.

As the descriptions contained in Chapter 5 indicate, strategy changes can also be a means of strengthening the dominant coalition in place, as new shareholders and managers who support the change are attracted to the firm, and existing shareholders and managers who oppose the change exit. This effect is more quickly felt in the publicly traded firm, where shareholder turnover can be almost instant, but it also can affect the privately held firm, where strategy changes can be a way of forcing out recalcitrant shareholders. From this perspective, it is clear that strategy changes should also be considered to be a part of the political struggle over who directs the firm. Even if the identities of shareholders and managers do not change following a change in strategy, the new direction of the firm invariably says something about who is in charge. PSA's 2012 decision to break with past practice and agree to an equity alliance with GM signals a loss of power for those (family) shareholders who had opposed such a move for so many years and a gain of power for those shareholders and managers who pushed for the internationalization of the firm and eventually held sway. For PSA, the alliance with

GM is not just a strategy change; it is also a change of the dominant coalition.

The rationality of strategic decisions

We have argued that strategic decisions are the outcome of the interaction of different interests – between and among management and shareholders – and that strategic decisions in turn impact the balance of forces in the firm. In doing so, we have simplified the analysis by leaving out other stakeholders, namely employees and government. Even this simplified description of reality, however, has painted a very political picture of decision-making in the firm. One might therefore conclude that we have a rather pessimistic view of the possibility of making rational decisions. This interpretation needs to be clarified.

First of all, the idea that the interaction of different interests "pollutes" the "purity" of strategic decision-making hearkens back to an older era when management was king and it was possible to clearly distinguish between strategy and governance and between ownership and control. This is the picture of the world as described by Berle and Means, who based their views on data of American listed firms from the first thirty years of the twentieth century. In those days and indeed for several decades after World War II, it was possible to assume that management always knew best. In recent years, quite a few observers have gone over to the other extreme, arguing that shareholders know best and that management should merely execute on delivering shareholder value.

In the general case, there can be no pure strategic decision, only a strategic decision that serves economic interests. How that economic interest is defined from among the variety of interests represented between and among managers and shareholders depends on the balance of forces that governs the firm. Ultimately, it is a matter of how realistic one wants to be whether or not one includes in the analysis the different interests at play in making decisions. We do not question the rationality of the strategic choice that is finally made, but we do question the idea that the choice is unique and determined by a single rational actor.

What is a "good" strategy? The only way to address this fundamental issue is to reflect upon what is good for the firm. If strategic decisions are the outcome of the interaction of different interests and if every change in strategy also has an impact on the governance of the firm, then one has to ask whether the good of the firm even has a place in a realistic and therefore necessarily political view of strategic decision-making. The answer is that the good of the firm does have a place in the political view we have presented. In order to see how the good of the firm can be understood in a political view, it is useful to consider four possible theses concerning the link between particular interests and the interest of the firm:

(1) The thesis of *neutrality*: in this, the thesis still most widely taught and referred to, the decision-maker finds the right strategy and the other stakeholders cannot but agree, because the strategy maximizes their interests.

(2) The thesis of *natural convergence*: in this thesis, the sum of the interests of all the stakeholders produces the interest of the firm; the idea is that the stakeholders are sufficiently rational to defend their interests, permitting the firm to grow and thereby satisfy the interests of all. In other words, there is a natural convergence between particular interests and the interest of the firm.

(3) The thesis of *political conflict*: here, the interests of shareholders and managers are multiple, and strategy is a focal point for struggles over power. This is the thesis that we have referred to repeatedly as the general case in this book, to indicate that one cannot assume neutrality or natural convergence. Here, the stakeholders in power serve the interest of the firm by defining

strategy in a way that ensures the firm's survival and, at the same time, satisfies their own interests.

(4) The thesis of the firm's *superior interest*: this thesis considers the firm as a community in its own right, independent of the interests of shareholders and managers. In other words, the evaluation of the interaction of stakeholders' different interests refers to the abstract interest of the firm, considered as an individual in its own right. Consistent with this thesis, legal theory in many countries has given the firm the status of a moral person as a way of solidifying the notion of the superior interest of the firm.

Only rarely does one refer to only one of these theses in discussing the interest of the firm, but it is good practice to define which thesis provides the basis of the argument one is making, for each one represents a different way of understanding the firm as a political arena.

(1) In the assumption of neutrality that has held sway over business schools and boardrooms for so many years, technical specialists carry the day, because they possess knowledge that is supposed to be neutral; strategy and governance are seen as independent.

(2) In the assumption of natural convergence, corporate governance is the outcome of a broad discussion that reveals how a strategic decision can maximize the interests of all stakeholders.

(3) In the assumption of political conflict, a strategic decision results from the interaction of different interests and represents the victory of one actor or set of actors over the others. The better the interests of those who win out contribute to maximizing the interest of the firm, the better the governance of the firm.

(4) In the assumption of superior interest, the logic of the thesis of political conflict is inverted; the general interest of the firm is taken as a starting point for defining the strategy that has the best chance of ensuring the survival of the firm and evaluating the corporate governance that best serves the firm.

These four theses are not unique to corporate governance, but can also be found in other fields where different interests confront each other in a political contest like countries or cities. In and of themselves, these theses are not original, but merely testify to the fact that the firm is a type of community of interaction of men and women with different interests.

How a firm makes decisions and which of the four theses it adopts depends on the culture and history of the individual firm as well as on the situation. It is important to know which of the theses of firm interest is in use at the firm if one wants to understand how its corporate governance works, for the thesis in use determines how decision-makers think and act: Are they neutral (thesis 1)? Do they seek consensus (thesis 2)? Will they engage in a confrontation over different particular interests (thesis 3)? Or will they accept evaluation according to the standard of a superior interest (thesis 4)? To a large extent, the thesis of firm interest in use establishes how the board of directors functions and how corporate governance plays out in practice, especially when strategic change is on the agenda. Independent directors, in particular, cannot exercise their designated role of guaranteeing the long-term survival of the firm without taking a personal stance on the thesis of firm interest.

II. Implications for practice, policy, and research

If strategy is considered in the abstract sense of rational choice, analysis will be limited to the economics of the alternatives on the table. Raising the question "strategy for whom?" leads to a thorough scrutiny of the main actors in the strategic decision-making process – shareholders, executives, and board members. As we have tried to show, ownership and/or management may not be unified, and the board of directors may or may not exercise any real influence. Nonetheless, recognizing the different values, methods, and structural positions of the shareholders and managers involved in the strategic decision-making process represents a first necessary step in determining the instrumental roles played by different interests in the making of strategy.

The framework for analysis presented in this book provides a basis for shareholders, executives, and board members to understand what strategy means to their counterparts in the decision-making process. By making the distinctions we propose among different types of executives, shareholders are better able to figure out which strategies will be defended by executives in office, and better able to anticipate which strategies will be preferred by new executives, and influence the process of executive selection accordingly. Similarly, by comprehending the variety of shareholders that we portray, executives are in a better position to maintain sufficient shareholder support to stay the course or to effect strategic change. Board members, finally, who recognize the dynamics behind the formation, preservation, and dissolution of dominant coalitions among shareholders and managers are in a better place to carry out their duties in upholding the long-term perspectives of the firm. In practice, strategy is subject to the will and the purpose of specific individuals or groups – the main actors in the drama of strategic decision-making can only benefit by incorporating the reality we describe into their analysis.

Point to watch: business schools and MBAs

Decades of MBA cohorts have been led to believe that strategy and ownership are separate topics, addressed by different models and independent of each other. At its worst, MBA education has ignored corporate governance completely, presenting the work of the manager as occurring in a vacuum. If, however, strategy and ownership are tightly interlinked, as we propose in this book, then it is absolutely necessary for students to gain an understanding of how corporate governance and the interaction of different interests shape strategic decisions. As remarked earlier, the concept of managing change, so important to the modern MBA curriculum, loses most of its meaning, if it is not understood in the context of the external forces that are driving or blocking change. Rather than treating different interests and contests for power over the corporation as nonexistent or taboo, MBA education needs to spell out the political dimensions of corporate life and teach students how to anticipate and address them.

If shareholders and executives use strategy as a focal point to defend their own interests in the firm, then the views of supposedly neutral advisors involved in the strategic decision-making process should also be studied more carefully. Are management consultants, for example, not often utilized to strengthen the positions of executives, and *a fortiori*, the strategies they espouse? By the same token, legal advisors and auditors may also be working for one party or another, with the (often) unspoken objective of defending one strategy over another. Given the evidence presented in this book, it would seem that management consultants, legal advisors, and auditors would be well advised to carefully consider the views and positions of the different actors in the strategic decision-making process, to ensure that their work is not unwittingly biased. Board members seeking to advance the general good, in turn, need to do more to assess the allegiances of the firm's advisors. In general, these advisors are an integral part of the political struggle over strategy, and it would be naïve of any of the actors involved to think otherwise.

Point to watch: allegiances of advisors

Seeing advisors – consultants of various kinds, bankers, lawyers, accountants, and auditors – as part of a broader political process in strategic decision-making complicates the analysis, but also makes it more robust to unwanted influencing. Board members, in particular, are well advised to consider the motivation of the source of expert opinion. Of course, deal-makers will be pushing for more deals, and guardians of compliance will be pushing for more compliance, but the really interesting constellations occur when advisors are working with managers and shareholders to reinforce or upset the dominant coalition. At a minimum, decision-makers should understand the nature of the relationships between advisors and people connected to the firm.

Extending the analysis beyond ownership and management to include secondary players like advisors makes clear that the interplay of strategy and governance does not happen in a vacuum and, if a sufficient number of firms are implicated, can have a systemic effect. The Sarbanes-Oxley legislation of 2003 that changed the regulatory context for the executives of publicly listed companies and their auditors in the United States arose from a broad review of this very question. In a whole string of cases, executives and auditors had joined forces to hide important information from shareholders, resulting in heavy stock market losses, once the discrepancies became apparent. This is but one example of how the interplay of particular interests in business can affect the well-being of the economic system and the health of individual industries. As described in Chapter 3, the change in ownership form of the major US investment banks led these firms to pursue more risky strategies, in line with the interests of certain shareholders and certain executives, and these risky strategies eventually affected the entire economy. Had this effect been anticipated, regulators may not have been as sanguine about letting the firms in question collectively go public. In general, whenever entire industries or sectors appear to be driven by one particular interest over another, regulators need to pay attention, because this is the kind of development that can lead to extreme swings in the affected parts of the economy.

Decision-makers, whether they are in policy or in business, depend to some degree on research to provide the bases upon which to justify change. Since research in governance and research in strategy have largely pursued separate paths, the question of "strategy for whom?" has not received the attention its practical significance would warrant. Where multiple interests are involved in a struggle over who directs the firm and where there are distinct alternatives to be considered in deciding upon the direction of the firm, an interdisciplinary approach that combines the methods of political science and the models of economics appears most promising. Specifically, research needs to identify the different actors and interests involved in decision-making and track how they affect strategic choices and economic results over time in a variety of institutional contexts. This would give government, ownership, and management, a more nuanced picture of what is good for the individual actors, what is good for the firm, and what is good for the economy.

As we have shown, governance and strategy are inextricably linked, and if decision-makers ignore this link, the firm may ultimately be put in jeopardy. Since the work of Berle and Means and especially since the advent of finance departments and strategy departments in business schools in the 1960s and 1970s, the two fields have been thought about and taught as distinct. This was a comfortable fiction that stood the empirical test for many years (at least in the case of publicly listed firms in the United States). Bringing the two together again raises the difficult question of "strategy for whom?" This book represents an attempt to set out a framework for studying and answering this question. Our hope is that practice, policy, and research will benefit.

Background reading – Part IV

Huse, M. *Boards, Governance, and Value Creation*, Cambridge University Press, 2007.

MacMillan, I. C. *Strategy Formulation: Political Concepts*, St. Paul: West, 1978.

Mintzberg, H., Ahlstrand, B., and Lampel, J. *Strategy Safari*, New York: Free Press, 1998.

Monks, R. A. G and Minow, N. *Watching the Watchers*, Cambridge, MA: Blackwell Publishers, 1996.

Schendel, D. E. and Hofer, C. W. (eds.) *Strategic Management*, Boston: Little, Brown, 1979.

Notes

Introduction

1 Our summary description of this case draws on the Harvard Business School case study, *Deutsche Börse and the European Markets*, 9–206–082.

2 R. P. Rumelt, *Good Strategy Bad Strategy*, New York: Crown Business, 2011.

3 A. A. Berle and G. C. Means, *The Modern Corporation and Private Property*, New York: Transaction Publishers, 1932.

4 E. F. Fama and M. C. Jensen, Separation of Ownership and Control, *Journal of Law and Economics* 26 (2), 1983: 301–325.

5 M. J. Roe, *Strong Managers, Weak Owners: The Political Roots of American Corporate Finance*, Princeton University Press, 1994. In the literature, the shareholder-focused Anglo-American model of corporate governance is frequently opposed to the stakeholder-focused German and Japanese models; see T. E. Donaldson and L. E. Preston, The Stakeholder Theory of Corporation: Concepts, Evidence, and Implications, *Academy of Management Review* 20 (1), 1995: 68–91; S. Letza, X. Sun, and J. Kirkbride, Shareholding Versus Stakeholding: A Critical Review of Corporate Governance, *Corporate Governance: An International Review* 12 (3), 2004: 242–262.

6 P.-Y. Gomez and H. Korine, *Entrepreneurs and Democracy: A Political Theory of Corporate Governance*, Cambridge University Press, 2008, Chapters 5 and 6.

7 For an early treatment of the complexities arising from conflicting interests when ownership is heterogeneous, see H. Hansmann, Ownership of the Firm, *Journal of Law, Economics, & Organization* 4 (2), 1988: 267–304. For more recent work along these lines, see A. Werder, Corporate Governance and Stakeholder Opportunism, *Organization Science* 22 (5), 2011: 1345–1358. The research of P. David, J. P. O'Brien, T. Yoshikawa, and A. Delios, Do Shareholders or Stakeholders Appropriate the Rents from Corporate Diversification? The Influence of Ownership Structure, *Academy of Management Journal* 53 (3), 2010: 636–654, explores how different interests

among various shareholders (and stakeholders) play out empirically. For a discussion of different types of institutional investors, see L. Ryan and M. Schneider, Institutional Investor Power and Heterogeneity: Implications for Agency and Stakeholder Theories, *Business and Society* 42, 2003: 398–429.

8 Cf. M. A. Carpenter, M. A. Geletkanycz, and W. G. Sanders, Upper Echelons Research Revisited: Antecedents, Elements, and Consequences of Top Management Team Composition, *Journal of Management* 30, 2004: 749–778; B. J. Olsen, S. Parayitam, and Y. Bao, Strategic Decision Making: The Effects of Cognitive Diversity, Conflict, and Trust on Decision Outcomes, *Journal of Management* 33 (2), 2007: 196–222.

9 The work of S. Thomsen and T. Pedersen, Ownership Structure and Economic Performance in the Largest European Companies, *Strategic Management Journal* 21, 2000: 689–705, represents an important exception to the general dearth of literature on the relationship between ownership and strategy. Although their analysis is static, their argument that certain types of shareholders are better suited to certain kinds of strategies suggests the validity of a dynamic approach.

10 Cf. R. A. G. Monks and N. Minow, *Corporate Governance* (second edn.), Oxford: Blackwell, 2001; J. Solomon and A. Solomon, *Corporate Governance and Accountability*, Chichester: Wiley, 2004.

11 Cf. www.ecgi.de/codes/all_codes.php; note that in the United States the board of directors is supposed to act in the best long-term interests of *shareholders*, rather than the firm. The origins of this distinction are addressed in further detail in Chapter 8.

12 Gomez and Korine, *Entrepreneurs and Democracy*.

13 As discussed in foundational texts of the field such as P. Hofer and D. Schendel, *Strategy Formulation: Analytical Concepts*, St. Paul: West Publishing Company, 1978; M. Porter, *Competitive Strategy*, New York: Free Press, 1980; and R. P. Rumelt, Towards a Strategic Theory of the Firm, in R. B. Lamb (ed.), *Competitive Strategic Management*, Englewood Cliffs, NJ: Prentice-Hall, 1984, pp. 556–570.

1 Change in ownership

1 www.fundinguniverse.com/company-histories/Preussag-AG-company-History.html/.

2 B. Schigulski, *Die strategische Umstrukturierung einer Aktiengesellschaft. Eine gesellschafts-rechtliche Analyse des Wandels der Preussag AG zur TUI AG*, Jena: Jenaer Wissenschaftliche Verlags-gesellschaft mbH, 2010.

3 B. Stier and J. Laufer, *Von der Preussag zur TUI: Wege und Wandlungen eines Unternehmens 1923–2003*, Essen: Klartext, 2005.

4 A. von Werder, Corporate Governance and Stakeholder Opportunism, *Organization Science* 22 (5), 2011: 1345–1358.

5 See P. David, J. P. O'Brien, T. Yoshikawa, and A. Delios, Do Shareholders or Stakeholders Appropriate the Rents from Corporate Diversification? The Influence of Ownership Structure, *Academy of Management Journal* 53 (3), 2010: 636–654.

6 See L. Ryan and M. Schneider, Institutional Investor Power and Heterogeneity: Implications for Agency and Stakeholder Theories, *Business and Society* 42, 2003: 398–429.

7 For an economic treatment of the difference between vocal (active) and silent (passive) ownership, see the work of J. Willner and D. Parker, The Performance of Public and Private Enterprise under Conditions of Active and Passive Ownership and Competition and Monopoly, *Journal of Economics* 90 (3), 2007: 221–253. Depending on size of the corporate holding in relation to size of the portfolio, time horizon of investment, and nature of the fund, some types of institutional investors are likely to be more vocal (active) than others; see M. J. Roe, *Strong Managers, Weak Owners: The Political Roots of American Corporate Finance*, Princeton University Press, 1994; but also L. Ryan and M. Schneider, The Antecedents of Institutional Investor Activism, *Academy of Management Review* 27, 2002: 554–573; and D. Del Guercio and J. Hawkins, The Motivation and Impact of Pension Fund Activism, *Journal of Financial Economics* 52, 1999: 293–340.

8 For a broad treatment of the differences between the different types of shareholders, see P.-Y. Gomez and H. Korine, *Entrepreneurs and Democracy: A Political Theory of Corporate Governance*, Cambridge University Press, 2008, pp. 156–172.

9 See N. C. Churchill and K. J. Hatten, Non-market Based Transfers of Wealth and Power: A Research Framework of Family Business, *Family Business Review* 10 (1), 1997: 53–67. See also Chapter 5 of R. S. Carlock and J. L. Ward, *Strategic Planning for the Family Business*, London: Palgrave Macmillan, 2001.

10 Comments made in conversation with Harry Korine, 2010. On February 5, 2013, Pictet and Lombard Odier, two of the oldest Swiss private banks, announced that they would be revising their legal structure effective 2014, changing from a partnership with unlimited personal liability of the partners to a limited liability corporation. This change is to be seen in light of the increased size and complexity of the firms and the associated risk, a financial risk that today is too great for individuals to be personally held liable for. Although the legal structure will be different, the managing partners will still be the sole shareholders in the two firms.

11 W. D. Cohan, *The Last Tycoons: The Secret History of Lazard Frères & Co.*, New York: Doubleday, 2007.

12 For an innovative and highly successful practical approach to addressing the family member as nonexecutive owner, see the history of Merck, as described in the IMD case study, *The Mercks of Darmstadt: What Family Can Do*, IMD-3–3126, 2011.

13 A. R. Palmiter, Mutual Fund Voting of Portfolio Shares: Why Not Disclose? *Cardozo Law Review* 23 (4), 2002: 1419–1491. See also A. R. Admati and P. Pfleiderer, The "Wall Street Walk" and Shareholder Activism: Exit as a Form of Voice, *The Review of Financial Studies* 22 (7), 2009: 2645–2685.

14 B. G. Malkiel, *A Random Walk Down Wall Street: The Time-tested Strategy for Successful Investing*, New York: W. W. Norton, 1973.

15 For background, see the classics on growth and value investing, respectively, P. A. Fisher, *Common Stocks and Uncommon Profits*, New York: Harper & Bros., 1958; and B. Graham and D. Dodd, *Security Analysis* (sixth edn.), New York: McGraw-Hill Professional, 2008.

16 For an early treatment of this point, see G. Day and L. Fahey, Valuing Market Strategies, *Journal of Marketing* 52 (3), 1988: 45–57.

17 For a general treatment of the mechanisms behind these effects, see B. M. Staw and L. D. Epstein, What Bandwagons Bring: Effects of Popular Management Techniques on Corporate Performance, Reputation, and CEO Pay, *Administrative Science Quarterly* 45 (6), 2000: 523–556; and, for a focus on the role of the board, H. Korine, M. Alexander, and P.-Y. Gomez, The Real Job of Boards, *Business Strategy Review* 21 (3), 2010: 36–41.

18 M. Becht, J. Franks, C. Mayer, and S. Rossi, Returns to Shareholder Activism: Evidence from a Clinical Study of the Hermes UK Focus Fund, *Review of Financial Studies* 23 (3), 2010: 3093–3129.

19 L. Alfaro and R. Kim, Sovereign Wealth Funds: For Profits/Politics, *Harvard Business School Note*, 2008.

20 www.dentsu.com/ir/data/annual/2011/pdf/EAR_g_all.pdf/.

21 For a comprehensive review of the literature on managerial compensation, see M. Goergen and L. Reneboog, Managerial Compensation, *Journal of Corporate Finance* 17 (4), 2011: 1068–1077. The use of stock options is chronicled in C. Frydman and R. E. Saks, Executive Compensation: A New View from a Long-term Perspective, 1936–2005, *Review of Financial Studies* 23, 2010: 2099–2138.

22 The full theoretical argument is presented in P.-Y. Gomez and H. Korine, The Firm as a Nexus of Promises, Paper presented at the annual EURAM meetings in Rome, May 2010. Recent empirical work has shown that the presence of institutional investors increased the riskiness of banks during the subprime financial crisis: L. Laeven and R. Levine, Bank Governance, Regulation, and Risk-Taking, *Journal of Financial Economics* 93 (2), 2009: 259–75; A. Ellul and V. Yerramilli, *Stronger Risk Controls, Lower Risk:*

Evidence from U. S. Bank Holding Companies, Mimeo, Indiana University, 2010.

2 Change in management

1 The more general question the finance literature has addressed is whether or not CEOs really have an independent effect on firm performance, taking the event of a change in CEO as a basis for investigating performance differences. See Y. Y. Chang, S. Dasgupta, and G. Hilary, CEO Ability, Pay, and Firm Performance, *Management Science* 56 (10), 2010: 1633–1652, for a recent study that shows that the CEO does indeed matter for firm performance. For a broader treatment of the relationship between organizational performance and executive succession, see D. Miller, Stale in the Saddle: CEO Tenure and the Match Between Organization and Environment, *Management Science* 37, 1991: 34–52.

2 M. Bertrand and A. Schoar, Managing with Style: The Effect of Managers on Firm Policies, *Quarterly Journal of Economics* 118, 2003: 1169–1208.

3 R. M. Kanter, Leadership and the Psychology of Turnarounds, *Harvard Business Review* 81 (6), 2003: 58–67. It needs to be pointed out, however, that the research evidence on performance turnaround following CEO change is inconclusive; see G. J. Castrogiovanni, B. R. Baliga, and R. E. Kidwell, Jr., Curing Sick Businesses: Changing CEOs in Turnaround Efforts, *Academy of Management Executive* 6 (3), 1992: 26–41.

4 For a descriptive account of the process of CEO succession, see R. M. Vancil, *Passing the Baton: Managing the Process of CEO Succession*, Cambridge, MA: Harvard Business School Press, 1987. The institutionalist approach of Ocasio helps explain when firms choose insiders over outsiders and reinforces the importance of this distinction; see W. Ocasio, Institutionalized Action and Corporate Governance: The Reliance on Rules of CEO Succession, *Administrative Science Quarterly* 44 (2), 1999: 384–416.

5 The question of CEOs not turning out to be what they seem has a lot to do with how the board forms perceptions. Interestingly, this issue has been treated more extensively in the CEO dismissal literature. J. W. Frederickson, D. C. Hambrick, and S. Baumrin, A Model of CEO Dismissal, *Academy of Management Review* 13 (2), 1988: 255–270, provides a discussion of the importance of board expectations and attributions in prompting CEO dismissal. This approach is further refined to include board sense making and interpretation in J. Haleblian and R. Nandini, A Cognitive Model of CEO Dismissal: Understanding the Influence of Board Perceptions, Attributions and Efficacy Beliefs, *Journal of Management Studies* 43 (5), 2006: 1009–1026.

6 In defining executive methods as rupture or continuity, we draw on multiple sources, ranging from the concept of Maximum Man and Minimum Man, as described by A. Zaleznik and M. F. R. Kets de Vries, *Power and the Corporate Mind*, Boston: Houghton Mifflin, 1975, to the notion of managerial discretion underlined by D. C. Hambrick and S. Finkelstein, Managerial Discretion: A Bridge between Polar Views of Organizational Outcomes, in L. L. Cummings and B. M. Staw (eds.), *Research in Organizational Behavior*, 9, Greenwich, CT: JAI Press, 1987, pp. 369–406. Recent work has shown that methods can have a variety of psychological underpinnings: A. Chatterjee and D. C. Hambrick, It's All About Me: Narcissistic Chief Executive Officers and Their Effects on Company Strategy and Performance, *Administrative Science Quarterly* 52, 2007: 351–386.

7 Our discussion of values for CEOs is related to the literature on CEO mindsets that looks at the focus of attention of senior executives, distinguishing between an external and an internal focus: i.e., W. Ocasio, Towards an Attention-Based View of the Firm, *Strategic Management Journal* 18, 1997: 187–206; M. S. Yadav, J. C. Prabhu, and R. K. Chandy, Managing the Future: CEO Attention and Innovation Outcomes, *Journal of Marketing* 71, 2007: 84–101. Whereas this literature highlights the fact that many CEOs have an external focus of attention, we underline the distinction and emphasize the existence of both types, sometimes even in the same TMT (top management team).

8 These cases are described in more detail in M. A. Alexander and H. Korine, When You Shouldn't Go Global, *Harvard Business Review* 86 (12), 2008: 70–77; and H. Korine, M. A. Alexander, and P.-Y. Gomez, The Real Job of Boards, *Business Strategy Review* 21 (3), 2010: 36–41.

9 Cf. A. C. Amason, Distinguishing the Effects of Functional and Dysfunctional Conflict on Strategic Decision Making: Resolving a Paradox for Top Management Teams, *Academy of Management Journal* 39, 1996: 123–148. The more general point that top management teams often disagree was first made in D. C. Hambrick and P. Mason, Upper Echelons: The Organization as a Reflection of the Top Managers, *Academy of Management Review* 9, 1984: 193–206, and elaborated in D. C. Hambrick, Top Management Groups: A Conceptual Integration and Reconsideration of the "Team" Label, *Research in Organizational Behavior* 6, 1994: 171–214, and D. C. Hambrick, Fragmentation and the Other Problems CEOs Have with Their Top Management Teams, *California Management Review* 37 (3), 1995: 110–127.

10 For background on the relationship between the performance history and the future success of CEOs, see C. E. Fee and C. J. Hadlock, Raids, Rewards, and Reputations in the Market for Managerial Talent, *Review*

of Financial Studies 16, 2003: 1315–1357, and I. S. Fulmer, The Elephant in the Room: Labor Market Influences on CEO Compensation, *Personnel Psychology* 62, 2009: 659–695.

11 See Hambrick and Mason, Upper Echelons, which emphasized the importance of CEO experience in predicting CEO actions. Subsequent research by Hambrick and others has borne this out, although the relationship has been shown to be subject to numerous moderating effects that make linear predictions dangerous, cf. G. A. Bigley and M. F. Wiersema, New CEOs and Corporate Strategic Refocusing: How Experience as Heir Apparent Influences the Use of Power, *Administrative Science Quarterly* 47, 2002: 707–727.

12 Cf. R. P. Beatty and E. J. Zajac, Managerial Incentives, Monitoring, and Risk Bearing: A Study of Executive Compensation, Ownership, and Board Structure in Initial Public Offerings, *Administrative Science Quarterly* 39, 1994: 313–335; E. J. Zajac and J. D. Westphal, The Costs and Benefits of Managerial Incentives and Monitoring in Large US Corporations: When Is More Not Better? *Strategic Management Journal* 15, 1994: 121–142.

13 This question is also asked in D. C. Hambrick, Upper Echelons Theory: An Update, *Academy of Management Review* 32 (3), 2007: 334–343.

14 O. Bandiera, L. Guiso, A. Prat, and R. Sadun, Matching Firms, Managers, and Incentives, Harvard Business School Working Paper 10–073, 2011.

15 For a careful study of how the personal investment of the CEO affects the strategic activity of the company (in the case of acquisitions), see U. Malmendier and G. Tate, Who Makes Acquisitions? CEO Overconfidence and the Market's Reaction, *Journal of Financial Economics* 89 (1), 2008: 20–43.

16 For a recent discussion and empirical treatment of this issue, see K. Chen, Y.-C. Kim, and R. D. Marcus, Hands in the Cookie Jar? The Case of Management Buyouts, *International Review of Accounting, Banking & Finance* 3 (1), 2011: 43–69.

17 For a more general discussion of this point, see Chapter 1, note 22. The percentage of UBS shares held by the two principal clearing organizations for institutional investors, Chase Nominees Ltd., London, and DTC (Cede & Co.), New York, The Depository Trust Company, dropped from 22.14 at the end of 2007 to 17.39 as of June 30, 2011 and 17.51 as of September 30, 2011 (taken from www.ubs.com).

18 www.businessweek.com/managing/content/sep2008/ca2008099_190182. htm; www.startribune.com/printarticle/?id=13571511/.

19 For a practical approach to making CEO succession an integral part of corporate governance, see R. Charan, Ending the CEO Succession Crisis, *Harvard Business Review* 83 (2), 2005: 72–81, and for a study on the

condition of CEO succession planning, S. A. Miles and D. F. Larcker, Do You Have a Plan for Finding Your Next CEO? *Corporate Board* 31 (184), 2010: 11–15.

20 See P.-Y. Gomez and H. Korine, *Entrepreneurs and Democracy: A Political Theory of Corporate Governance*, Cambridge University Press, 2008, for a more detailed discussion of this point.

21 www.bloomberg.com/apps/news?pid=newsarchive&sid=av0oK2D8zQgg/.

22 A. Shleifer and R. W. Vishny, Management Entrenchment: The Case of Manager-Specific Investments, *Journal of Financial Economics* 25, 1989: 123–139.

3 Change in legal structure

1 As Holderness showed, this generalization holds across countries, including the United States. C. G. Holderness, The Myth of Diffuse Ownership in the United States, *The Review of Financial Studies* 22, 2009: 1377–1408.

2 The nationalization of both privately held and publicly listed firms obeys a political logic of national interest that predominates in times of war or political/economic instability. We have chosen not to cover this category of change of ownership form in this book and refer the reader to the extensive literatures on nationalization in economic history and political science.

3 See M. Lewis, The End of Wall Street's Boom, *Portfolio*, November 11, 2008.

4 Weakened by suits following charges of market manipulation in the trading of US government bonds, Salomon Brothers had been absorbed in 1998 by the much larger Travelers.

5 See A. Greenberg and M. Singer, *The Rise and Fall of Bear Stearns*, New York: Simon & Schuster, 2010.

6 J. A. Knee, *The Accidental Investment Banker*, New York: Random House, 2006.

7 This point is emphasized in the account of Peter J. Solomon, former Lehman Brothers partner and founder of the eponymous boutique investment bank (cited in *The Deal*, July 23, 2007, pp. 46–48, 58–59).

8 Cf. Were Investment Bank IPOs Really the Problem?, *The Atlantic Monthly*, January, 2009.

9 Cf. J. Surowiecki, Public Humiliation, *The New Yorker*, September 29, 2008.

10 P. Espinasse, *IPO: A Global Guide*, 2011, www.ipo-book.com/blog/2011/03/.

11 See also R. Morck, A. Shleifer, and R. W. Vishny, The Stock Market and Investment: Is the Market a Sideshow? *Brookings Papers on Economic Activity*, 2, 1990: 157–215, who argue that the ownership form decision is

a stock market-driven "sideshow" without any effect on investment (read strategy) and profits.

12 Interview in *Financial Times*, January 26, 2011.

13 www.microfinancefocus.com/news/2010/05/17/exclusive-sks-microfinance-journey-to-ipo-an-inside-story/.

14 www.businessweek.com/news/2011-11-24/sks-to-add-financial-services-to-microfinance-as-founder-quits.html/.

15 Cf. J. Blas, Out of the Shadows, *Financial Times*, April 11, 2011.

16 www.baselinemag.com/c/a/Projects-Processes/Compliance-How-BearingPoint-Lost-Its-Way/2/.

17 www.highbeam.com/doc/1G1-138726681.html; www.rusmergers.com/en/mna/4152-.html/.

18 M. Pagano, The Flotation of Companies on the Stock Market: A Coordination Failure Model, *European Economic Review* 37, 1993: 1101–1125. M. Pagano, F. Panetta, and L. Zingales, Why Do Companies Go Public? An Empirical Analysis, *Journal of Finance* 53, 1998: 27–64. For an integrative discussion, see H. Aslan and P. Kumar, Lemons or Cherries? Growth Opportunities and Market Temptations in Going Public and Private, *Journal of Financial and Quantitative Analysis* 46 (2), 2011: 489–526.

19 *Preparing for the Google IPO: A Revolution in the Making?* IMD case study IMD-1-0216, 2004.

20 P. N. Giraud, Les fonds de pension – vers un nouveau capitalisme? CERNA, *Revue Etudes Tome* 394 (2), 2001, www.cerna.ensmp.fr/Documents/PNG-EtudesFev01.pdf.

21 M. Jensen, Agency Costs of Free Cash Flow, Corporate Finance and Takeovers, *American Economic Review* 76, 1986: 323–339; K. Lehn and A. Poulsen, Free Cash Flow and Stockholder Gains in Going Private Transactions, *The Journal of Finance* 44 (3), 1989: 771–787.

22 See Aslan and Kumar, Lemons or Cherries? for an interesting demonstration (based on post-transaction data) of the importance of agency costs in precipitation the going private decision.

23 The February 5, 2013 announcement that Dell Corporation would be taken private by Michael Dell and a group of associated investors including Microsoft and Silver Lake (a major private equity firm) follows the same pattern: necessary, but difficult decisions about how to refocus the strategy of Dell are easier if there are only a small number of decision-makers who have agreed on the way forward.

24 Note that we do not treat here the case of a publicly listed firm being taken over or merged into another publicly listed firm. This is the most common case of delisting, but it does not take the focal firm private. For a comprehensive overview of the recent history of delisting in one country (France), see P.-Y. Gomez and Z. Guedri, Pourquoi sort-on de la Bourse?

Preuves à l'Appui, Institut Français de Gouvernement des Entreprises, Cahier No. 2, 2012.

25 Cf. Aslan and Kumar, Lemons or Cherries? and S. Guo, E. S. Hotchkiss, and W. Song, Do Buyouts (Still) Create Value? *Journal of Finance* 66 (2), 2011: 479–517.

26 P. R. Haunschild, How Much is that Company Worth? Interorganizational Relationships, Uncertainty, and Acquisition Premiums, *Administrative Science Quarterly* 39, 1994: 391–411.

4 Change in organizational structure

1 In other words, not only does structure follow strategy, but strategy also follows structure. This insight was originally proposed by D. J. Hall and M. A. Salas, Strategy Follows Structure! *Strategic Management Journal* 1, 1980: 149–163, and further developed by R. A. Burgelman, A Model of the Interaction of Strategic Behavior, Corporate Context, and the Concept of Strategy, *Academy of Management Review* 8, 1983: 61–70.

2 This is what Galunic and Eisenhardt refer to as "organizational form" and "formal processes" in their review of the literature: C. A. Galunic and K. M. Eisenhardt, Renewing the Strategy–Structure–Performance Paradigm, *Research in Organizational Behavior* 16, 1994: 215–255. In order not to stray too far, we do not cover informal structure, culture, and values in this chapter; clearly these characteristics of organization also have an impact on strategy.

3 This point is described as "the time-honored cycle between centralization and decentralization" in R. G. Eccles and N. Nohria, *Beyond the Hype: Rediscovering the Essence of Management*, Cambridge, MA: HBS Press, 1992:127; and as "analytically developed" in J. A. Nickerson and T. R. Zenger, Being Efficiently Fickle: A Dynamic Theory of Organizational Choice, *Organization Science* 13, 2002: 547–566. In the case of public administration, the observation that phases of decentralization and phases of centralization appear to alternate was first made by Kaufman, in H. Kaufman, Administrative Decentralization and Political Power, in J. M. Shafritz and A. C. Hyde (eds.), *Classics of Public Administration* (fourth edn., pp. 289–301), Belmont, CA: Wadsworth, 1997 (original work published 1969).

4 This thesis was first presented in A. Chandler, *Strategy and Structure: Chapters in the History of the American Industrial Enterprise*, Cambridge, MA: MIT Press, 1962.

5 See H. D. Korine and A.G. Fresenius, High-Speed Globalization, *Business Strategy Review* 11, 2000: 47–57.

6 J. Cassidy, The Firm, *The New Yorker*, March 8, 1999, p. 30.

7 M. Beer, R. A. Eisenstat, and B. Spector, Why Change Programs Don't Produce Change, *Harvard Business Review* 68, 1990: 158–166.

8 For an interesting empirical study of this effect, see J. B. Thomas and R. R. McDaniel, Jr., Interpreting Strategic Issues: Effects of Strategy and the Information Processing Structure of Top Management Teams, *Academy of Management Journal* 33, 1990: 286–306.

9 For a summary description of management control processes as they relate to organization and strategy, see R. L. Daft and N. B. Macintosh, The Nature and Use of Formal Control Systems for Management Control and Strategy Implementation, *Journal of Management* 10, 1984: 43–66.

10 This effect is described and analyzed in S. F. Borde, J. Madura, and A. Akhigbe, Valuation Effects of Foreign Divestitures, *Managerial and Decision Economics* 19, 1998: 71–79.

11 A broad-based discussion of the implications of restructuring is provided in B. Lin, Z.-H. Lee, and R. Peterson, An Analytical Approach for Making Management Decisions Concerning Corporate Restructuring, *Managerial and Decision Economics* 27, 2006: 655–666.

12 See Chapter 8 of O. Williamson, *Markets and Hierarchies*, New York: Free Press, 1975.

13 For an overview, see J. R. Galbraith, *Designing Matrix Organizations That Actually Work: How IBM, Procter & Gamble, and Others Design for Success*, San Francisco: Jossey-Bass, 2009.

14 For an interesting theoretical discussion of the risk implications of centralization and decentralization, see A. Arcuri and G. Dari-Mattiacci, Centralization versus Decentralization as a Risk-Return Trade-Off, *Journal of Law & Economics* 53, 2010: 359–378.

15 Instead of repeatedly changing organization structure, a number of authors have argued that it can be more effective to focus on adjusting management processes, e.g., C. A. Bartlett, and S. Ghoshal, MNCs: Get off the Reorganization Merry-go-round, *Harvard Business Review* 71, 1993: 138–147.

16 P. Killing, *Nestle's Globe Program (A): The Early Months*, IMD-3-1334, 2003.

17 This point is also made in R. G. Eccles, The Performance Measurement Manifesto, *Harvard Business Review* 69, 1991: 131–137. For a longitudinal account that shows how broadly corporate transformation efforts can affect the workings of an organization, see G. F. Gebhardt, G. S. Carpenter, and J. F. Sherry, Jr., Creating a Market Orientation: A Longitudinal, Multiform, Grounded Analysis of Cultural Transformation, *Journal of Marketing* 70, 2006: 37–55.

18 Private communication to the authors.

5 Corporate and business strategies

1 Cf. R. M. Grant, *Contemporary Strategy Analysis* (seventh edn.),
New York: Wiley, 2009.

2 J. D. Martin and A. Sayrak, Corporate Diversification and Shareholder
Value: A Survey of Recent Literature, *Journal of Corporate Finance*, 9 (1),
2003: 37–57 provides a summary of this literature.

3 See Introduction, note 13.

4 On average, related diversifiers have been found to outperform
unrelated diversifiers (cf. R. P. Rumelt, *Strategy, Structure, and Economic
Performance*, Boston: Harvard University, 1974; C. C. Markides and P. J.
Williamson, Related Diversification, Core Competences, and Corporate
Performance, *Strategic Management Journal* 15 (S2), 1994: 149–165),
but this result depends on the measures and conceptualization of
relatedness.

5 Cf. A. Campbell, M. Goold, and M. Alexander, Corporate Strategy: The
Quest for Parenting Advantage, *Harvard Business Review*, March–April,
1995: 120–132.

6 A. Shleifer and R. W. Vishny, Management Entrenchment: The Case of
Manager-Specific Investments, *Journal of Financial Economics* 25, 1989:
123–139. See also Part III, note 2.

7 Cf. S. A. Zahra and I. Filatotchev, Governance of the Entrepreneurial
Threshold Firm: A Knowledge-based Perspective, *Journal of Management
Studies* 41 (5), 2004: 885–897.

8 Cf. R. C. Anderson, T. W. Bates, J. M. Bizjak, and M. L. Lemmon,
Corporate Governance and Firm Diversification, *Financial Management* 29
(1), 2000: 5–22.

9 This is the case of the promoter-led firms in India, for example. See
R. Chakrabarti, W. Megginson, and P. K. Yadav, Corporate Governance in
India, *Journal of Applied Corporate Finance* 20 (1), 2008: 59–72.

10 Glencore's proposed merger with Xstrata (2012) is a recent example, a
case made all the more interesting by the fact that the merger was clearly
signaled to the markets and all prospective shareholders when Glencore
announced its IPO in 2011.

11 Presentation by Valerie Mars, for "Challenges in Corporate Governance,"
London Business School, London, 2010.

12 Presentation by Michael Hilti for "Neues VR-Management," Hochschule
St. Gallen, Zurich, 2009.

13 Cf. Chapter 1. See also H. Korine, *Hermes Pensions Management*, London
Business School case study, 2003.

14 F. López de Silanes, R. La Porta, and A. Shleifer, Corporate Ownership
Around the World, *Journal of Finance* 54 (2), 1999: 471–517.

15 This point has become a tenet of finance theory, cf. Y. Amihud and
B. Lev, Risk Reduction as a Managerial Motive for Conglomerate Mergers,
The Bell Journal of Economics 12 (2), 1981: 605–617. For a strategy-focused
discussion, see C. A. Montgomery, Corporate Diversification, *Journal of
Economic Perspectives* 8 (3), 1994: 163–178.

16 Korine, *Hermes Pensions Management.*

17 See Introduction and Chapter 1.

18 It is important to note that this effect does not hold at the country level
of analysis. Numerous studies have shown that the country effect overrides
forces for international convergence. Cf. C. Doidge, G. A. Karolyi, and
R. M. Stulz, Why Do Countries Matter so much for Corporate Governance?
Journal of Financial Economics 86, 2007: 1–39; T. Khanna, J. Kogan, and
K. Palepu, Globalization and Similarities in Corporate Governance:
A Cross-country Analysis, *Review of Economics and Statistics* 88, 2006: 69–90.

19 Cf. G. F. Davis and C. Marquis, The Globalization of Stock Markets
and Convergence in Corporate Governance, in V. Nee and R. Swedberg
(eds.), *The Economic Sociology of Capitalism*, Princeton University
Press, 2005, pp. 352–390. These authors emphasize the importance of
studying the organizational sociology of how governance changes with
globalization, at the firm level of analysis.

20 This point is discussed in R. M. Stulz, *Globalization of Equity Markets and
the Cost of Capital*, NBER Working Paper No. 7021, 1999.

21 The original case studies describing the globalization of these firms can
be found as K. Asakawa, P.-Y. Gomez, and H. Korine, *Renault/Nissan*,
London Business School, EM-Lyon, Keio Business School, 2000 (also
published in C. Bartlett, S. Ghoshal, and J. Birkinshaw, *Transnational
Management* (third edn.), New York: MacMillan, 2003, pp. 593–617);
H. Korine, *Fresenius A. G.*, London Business School and INSEAD, 1999
(also published in H.Korine, Fresenius A. G.: High-speed Globalization,
Business Strategy Review 11, 2, 2000); and H. Korine, *Bombardier, Inc.*,
London Business School, 1999.

22 Personal communication to the authors, Paris-Billancourt, 2000.

23 Fresenius Medical Care, *Annual Report 2010*, p. 24.

24 The most influential texts and reference articles in business strategy make
no mention of shareholders or of shareholders' influence on business
strategy. Cf. M. Porter, *Competitive Strategy*, New York: Free Press, 1980;
D. J. Teece, G. Pisano, and A. Shuen, Dynamic Capabilities and Strategic
Management, *Strategic Management Journal* 18 (7), 1997: 537–533. Quite
to the contrary, the role of managers continues to be highlighted by
leading scholars in the field, as in D. J. Teece, Dynamic Capabilities and
the Role of Managers in Business Strategy and Economic Performance,
Organization Science 20 (2), 2009: 410–421.

25 See J. Wiggins, The Inside Story of the Cadbury Takeover, *Financial Times Magazine*, March 12, 2010.

26 For a recent overview of the evidence on long/short funds, see W. Fung and D. A. Hsieh, The Risk in Hedge Fund Strategies: Theory and Evidence from Long/Short Equity Hedge Funds, *Journal of Empirical Finance* 18 (4), 2011: 547–569.

27 Cf. SAS/lepus, *Near Real-time Risk Management*, 2011, www.sas.com/reg/gen/uk/lepus.

28 Cf. R. M. Grant, *Contemporary Strategy Analysis* (seventh edn.), New York: Wiley, 2009; Teece et al., Dynamic Capabilities and Strategic Management.

29 Presentation to investor conference, September 4, 2003, by Josef Ackermann, spokesman of the Board of Managing Directors and chairman of the Group Executive Committee (Deutsche Bank).

30 The subsection on the difficulty of implementing new strategies draws extensively on the joint research of Harry Korine and Quy Huy.

31 See P. C. Nutt, Surprising but True: Half the Decisions in Organizations Fail, *Academy of Management Executive* 13 (4), 1999: 75–90; and D. J. Hickson, S. J. Miller, and D. C. Wilson, Planned or Prioritized? Two Options in Managing the Implementation of Strategic Decisions, *Journal of Management Studies* 40, 2003: 1803–1836.

32 See M. Useem, *Investor Capitalism: How Money Managers Are Changing the Face of Corporate America*, New York: Basic Books, 1996; and P. Aghion and J. Stein, Growth vs. Margins: Destabilizing Consequences of Giving the Stock Market What It Wants, *Journal of Finance* 63, 2008: 1025–1058.

33 This point is made in J. Stein, Rational Capital Budgeting in an Irrational World. *Journal of Business* 69, 1996: 429–455 and further developed in C. Polk and P.Sapienza, The Stock Market and Corporate Investment: A Test of Catering Theory, *The Review of Financial Studies* 22, 2009: 187–217.

34 Further material on these examples can be found in A. K. Kashyap, Lessons from the Financial Crisis for Risk Management, Paper prepared for the Financial Crisis Inquiry Commission, February 27, 2010 (on the management of trading risk); in B. G. Auguste, E. P. Harman, and V. Pandit, The Right Service Strategies for Product Companies, *The McKinsey Quarterly* 1, 2006: 41–51 (on the delivery of business consulting); and in M. A. Alexander and H. Korine, When You Shouldn't Go Global, *Harvard Business Review* 86 (12), 2008: 70–77 (on global coordination).

35 See E. Mosakowski, Strategy Making under Causal Ambiguity: Conceptual Issues and Empirical Evidence, *Organization Science* 8, 1997: 414–442; and A. W. King; and C. P. Zeithaml, Competencies and the Causal Ambiguity Paradox, *Strategic Management Journal* 22, 2001: 75–99; but also

S. W. Floyd and B. Wooldridge, Dinosaurs or Dynamos? Recognizing Middle Management's Strategic Role, *Academy of Management Executive* 8, 1994: 47–57.

36 D. A. Gioia and K. Chittipeddi, Sensemaking and Sensegiving in Strategic Change Initiation, *Strategic Management Journal* 12, 1991: 433–448; F. R. Westley, Middle Managers and Strategy: Microdynamics of Inclusion, *Strategic Management Journal* 11, 1990: 337–351; and I. Nonaka and H. Takeuchi, *The Knowledge-creating Company: How Japanese Companies Create the Dynamics of Innovation*, Oxford University Press, 1995.

37 See L. J. Bourgeois and D. R. Brodwin, Strategic Implementation: Five Approaches to an Elusive Phenomenon, *Strategic Management Journal* 5, 1984: 241–264; and G. Szulanski, Y. Doz, and J. Porac, Strategy Process: Introduction to the Volume, in G. Szulanski, Y. Doz, and J. Porac (eds.), *Advances in Strategic Management* (Vol. XXII), Bingley, UK: Emerald Group Publishing Limited, 2006: xiii–xxxv.

38 See J. W. Dean and M. P. Sharfman, Does Decision Process Matter? A Study of Strategic Decision-making Effectiveness, *Academy of Management Journal* 39, 1996: 368–396; Hickson et al., Planned or Prioritized?; C. H. Noble, The Eclectic Roots of Strategy Implementation Research, *Journal of Business Research* 45, 1999: 119–134; and J. R. Galbraith and R. K. Kazanjian, *Strategy Implementation: Structure, Systems, and Process* (second edn.), St. Paul, MN: West, 1986.

39 See Bourgeois and Brodwin, Strategic Implementation; R. L. Daft and N. B. Macintosh, The Nature and Use of Formal Control Systems for Management Control and Strategy Implementation, *Journal of Management* 10, 1984: 43–66; V. Govindarajan, A Contingency Approach to Strategy Implementation at the Business-unit Level: Integrating Administrative Mechanisms with Strategy, *Academy of Management Journal* 31, 1988: 828–853; and Nutt, Surprising but True.

40 See note 28 above; Nutt, Surprising but True; and Hickson et al., Planned or Prioritized?.

41 See J. E. Dutton and R. B. Duncan, The Influence of the Strategic Planning Process on Strategic Change, *Strategic Management Journal* 8, 1987: 103–116.

42 See Teece et al., Dynamic Capabilities and Strategic Management; and C. E. Helfat and M. A. Peteraf, The Dynamic Resource-based View: Capability Lifecycles, *Strategic Management Journal* 24, 2003: 997–1010.

43 See D. Miller and P. Friesen, *Organizations: A Quantum View*, Englewood Cliffs, NJ: Prentice-Hall, 1984; and R. Greenwood and C. R. Hinings, Understanding Radical Organizational Change: Bringing Together the Old and the New Institutionalism, *Academy of Management Review* 21, 1996: 1022–1054.

44 See J. V. Singh, R. J. House, and D. J. Tucker, Organizational Change and Organizational Mortality, *Administrative Science Quarterly* 31, 1986: 587–611; and D. C. Hambrick and R. D'Aveni, Large Corporate Failures as Downward Spirals, *Administrative Science Quarterly* 33, 1988: 1–23.

45 Hambrick and D'Aveni, Large Corporate Failures as Downward Spirals.

46 See Q. N. Huy, Emotional Balancing of Organizational Continuity and Radical Change: The Contribution of Middle Managers, *Administrative Science Quarterly* 47, 2002: 31–69.

47 On personal reasons such as hubris, see R. Roll, The Hubris Hypothesis of Corporate Takeovers, *Journal of Business* 59, 1986: 197–216; and M. L. A. Hayward and D. C. Hambrick, Explaining the Premiums Paid for Large Acquisitions: Evidence of CEO Hubris, *Administrative Science Quarterly* 42, 1997: 103–127. On the influence of external stakeholders, see M. Geletkanycz and D. C. Hambrick, The External Ties of Top Executives: Implications for Strategic Choice and Performance, *Administrative Science Quarterly* 42, 1997: 654–681.

48 The Carnegie School originated in the work of J. G. March and H. A. Simon, *Organizations*, New York: Wiley, 1958; and R. M. Cyert and J. G. March, *A Behavioral Theory of the Firm*, New Jersey: Prentice-Hall, 1963. On executive management and middle management working with different kinds of information, see B. Wooldridge, T. Schmid, and S. Floyd, The Middle Manager Perspective on Strategy Process: Contributions, Synthesis, and Future Research, *Journal of Management* 34, 2008: 1190–1221; A. M. L. Raes, M. G. Heijltjes, U. Glunk, and R. A. Roe, The Interface of the Top Management Team and Middle Managers: A Process Model, *Academy of Management Review* 36, 2011: 102–126. On having different aspects of the firm in focus, see W. Ocasio, Towards an Attention-based View of the Firm, *Strategic Management Journal* 18 (Summer Special Issue), 1997: 187–206; C. S. Tuggle, K. Schnatterly, and R. A. Johnson, Attention Patterns in the Boardroom: How Board Composition and Processes Affect Discussion of Entrepreneurial Issues, *Academy of Management Journal* 53, 2010: 550–571; and K. Rost and M. Osterloh, Opening the Black Box of Upper Echelons: Drivers of Poor Information Processing During the Financial Crisis, *Corporate Governance: An International Review* 18, 2010: 212–233.

49 On different interests, see W. D. Guth and I. C. MacMillan, Strategy Implementation versus Middle Management Self-interest, *Strategic Management Journal* 7, 1986: 313–327; and D. C. Hambrick, Upper Echelons Theory: An Update, *Academy of Management Review* 32, 2007: 334–343. On different identities, see Q. N. Huy, How Middle Managers' Group-focus Emotions and Social Identities Influence Strategy Implementation, *Strategic Management Journal* 32, 2011: 1387–1410.

50 See J. D. Westphal and E. J. Zajac, Who Shall Govern? CEO–board Power, Demographic Similarity, and New Director Selection, *Administrative Science Quarterly* 40, 1995: 60–83; and C. A. O'Reilly III and B. G. M. Main, Economic and Psychological Perspectives on CEO Compensation: A Review and Synthesis, *Industrial and Corporate Change* 19, 2010: 675–712.

51 See Westphal and Zajac, Who Shall Govern?; M. L. McDonald, P. Khanna, and J. D. Westphal, Getting Them to Think Outside the Circle: Corporate Governance, CEO's External Advice Networks, and Firm Performance, *Academy of Management Journal* 51 (3), 2008: 453–475; and M. L. McDonald and J. D. Westphal, Getting by with the Advice of Their Friends: CEOs' Advice Networks and Firms' Strategic Responses to Poor Performance, *Administrative Science Quarterly* 48, 2003: 1–32.

52 This argument is presented more fully in the recent work of Gomez: P.-Y. Gomez, *Le Travail Invisible: Enquête sur une Disposition*, Paris: François Bourin Editeur, 2013.

53 Nomura corporate governance report, 2010, www.nomuraholdings.com/jp/investor/cg/data/cg_report.pdf.

54 Cf. M. Nakamoto, Nomura CEO Steps Down Over Trading Scandal, FT.com, July 26, 2012.

55 For an interesting interview with Stephen Elop of Nokia and Steve Ballmer of Microsoft upon the signing of the alliance agreement, see www.bbc.co.uk/news/business-12427680/.

6 *Despite failure,* no change in ownership, management, or strategy

1 For a broad discussion of the antecedents and consequences of strategic persistence, see W. Grossman and A. A. Cannella, Jr., The Impact of Strategic Persistence on Executive Compensation, *Journal of Management* 32, 2006: 257–278.

2 The concentration of power in one person and the stalemate of powers are sources of inertia specific to the questions about ownership, management, and strategy addressed in this book. One can imagine many other sources of inertia that also contribute to perpetuating the divide between a firm's results in the marketplace and strategic change; see M. T. Hannan and J. Freeman, Structural Inertia and Organizational Change, *American Sociological Review* 49 (2), 1984: 149–164.

3 Cf. S. A. Zahra and I. Filatotchev, Governance of the Entrepreneurial Threshold Firm: A Knowledge-based Perspective, *Journal of Management Studies* 41 (5), 2004: 885–897.

4 L. Jong Bae, One Year after Chairman Lee's Resignation, No Significant Fault, But No Significant Achievement: Long Term Investment Stuck, April 21, 2009, www.ajnews.co.kr/view. jsp?newsId=20110105000281; B. Dong Jin, 6 Months after Chairman Lee's Return, What is Change in Samsung? Heavy Investment and Active Seeking of New Business Opportunities, September 27, 2010, http://news20.busan.com/news/newsController.jsp?subSectionId=1010 020000&newsId=20100927000094/.

5 As the example of Samsung above makes clear, concentration of power is not a question of firm size or firm age: given the right constellation, as outlined above, it can happen anywhere, in publicly listed firms as well as in private firms. The entrenchment literature referred to earlier (Chapter 2, note 22) makes this point convincingly in the case of US listed companies.

6 C. A. Bartlett, *Philips versus Matsushita: The Competitive Battle Continues*, Harvard Business Publishing, Ref. no. 9–910–410, 2009.

7 Cf. Y. Lambrecht and J. Lievens, Pruning the Family Tree: An Unexplored Path to Family Business Continuity and Family Harmony, *Family Business Review* 21 (4), 2008: 295–313.

8 H. Korine, K. Asakawa, and P.-Y. Gomez, Partnering with the Unfamiliar, *Business Strategy Review* 13 (2), 2002: 41–50.

9 See JAL Annual Reports, 2003, 2004, 2005, 2006, 2007, and 2008.

10 See, for example, J. P. Kotter, *Leading Change*, Cambridge, MA: Harvard Business School Press, 1996.

11 H. Korine, *Hermes Pensions Management*, London Business School, 2003; M. Beer and N. Noria, *Breaking the Code of Change*, Cambridge, MA: Harvard Business School Press, 2000.

12 Korine et al., Partnering with the Unfamiliar.

13 This way of looking at management's access to superior information as a potential means of resolving shareholder differences contrasts with that of finance theory which has tended to view information in the hands of management as a tool for self-enrichment, as in S. C. Myers and N. S. Majluf, Corporate Financing and Investment Decisions When Firms Have Information That Investors Do Not Have, *Journal of Financial Economics* 13(2), 1984: 187–221.

14 For an overview of the issues of inviting outsiders into the capital of family firms, see P. Z. Poutziouris, The Views of Family Companies on Venture Capital: Empirical Evidence from the UK Small to Medium-Size Enterprising Economy, *Family Business Review* 14 (3), 2001: 277–291; and N. Upton and W. Petty, Venture Capital Investment and US Family Business, *Venture Capital: An International Journal of Entrepreneurial Finance* 2 (1), 2000: 27–39.

15 See D. Miller and I. Le Breton-Miller, Family Governance and Firm
Performance: Agency, Stewardship, and Capabilities, *Family Business
Review* 19 (1), 2006: 73–87.

7 *Because of success,* reinforcement of ownership, management, and strategy

1 Thus, at the time of writing, the term "corporate governance fraud"
registers well over 12 million Google entries and "corporate governance
rules" almost 150 million.
2 See F. Gino and G. Pisano, Why Leaders Don't Learn from Success,
Harvard Business Review, April, 2011.
3 Whereas overconfidence and myopia are rooted in individual cognition
and thus refer in the first instance to senior decision-makers (see
J. E. Russo and P. J. H. Shoemaker, Managing Overconfidence, *Sloan
Management Review* 33 (2), 1992: 7–17; T. Levitt, Marketing Myopia,
Harvard Business Review 28, July–August, 1960: 45–56), inertia is an
organizational concept that has to do with processes and structures
in the firm (see M. T. Hannan and J. Reeman, Structural Inertia and
Organizational Change, *American Sociological Review* 49 (2), 1984:
149–164).
4 Our discussion here echoes that of Mintzberg in his description of the
"Entrepreneurial School of Strategic Management": H. Mintzberg,
Strategy Formation: Schools of Thought, in J. Fredrickson (ed.),
Perspectives on Strategic Management, New York: HarperCollins, 1990;
and in H. Mintzberg, B. Ahlstrand, and J. Lampel, *Strategy Safari*,
New York: Free Press, 1998. Like Mintzberg, we highlight the
attribution of organizational success to a single individual; our focus,
however, is on the consequences for governance, not on the ontology of
this approach.
5 See Shareholder Report on UBS's Write-Downs, April 18, 2008; Banking
Crisis: Dealing With the Failure of the UK Banks, House of Commons
Treasury Committee, 7th Report of Session 2008–2009.
6 For more background on these three companies' adherence to their
strategic formulae, see the following case studies: J. Weeks, *Culture and
Leadership at IBM*, INSEAD 404–104–1, 2004; K. Cool and D. Sorensen,
Toys 'R' Us in 1999, INSEAD 300–130–1, 2000; W. Chen and J. Gimeno,
*Nokia and the New Mobile Ecosystem: Competing in the Age of Internet Mobile
Convergence*, INSEAD 312–122–1, 2012.
7 J. K. Liker and T. N. Ogden, *Toyota Under Fire*, New York: McGraw-Hill,
2011.

8 The board of directors

1 The full text of the Report is available under www.ecgi.org/codes/
   documents/cadbury.pdf. Further elaboration on the question of director
   independence as first articulated in the Cadbury Report can be found
   under www.iod.com/MainWebSite/Resources/Document/roleofnxds_1006.
   pdf.
2 As described in R. A. G. Monks and N. Minow, *Corporate Governance*,
   Cambridge, MA: Blackwell Publishers, 1995: 399–411.
3 The following definitions of the role of the board of directors in different
   jurisdictions are taken from www.ecgi.de/codes/all_codes.php.
4 In Germany, the supervisory board of firms with more than 2,000
   employees must include an equal number of representatives of capital
   and labor (one-third employee representatives in firms with 500–2,000
   employees); this is supposed to ensure that the principal stakeholders
   are treated equally. In practice, employee representatives often side
   with management, especially on questions that relate to maintaining
   employment, cf. G. Gorton and F. Schmid, Capital, Labor, and the Firm:
   A Study of German Codetermination, *Journal of the European Economic
   Association* 2, 2004: 863–905. However, the effect on firm performance of
   employee representatives on the board ultimately depends on how they
   are made use of, cf. L. Fauver and M. E. Fuerst, Does Good Corporate
   Governance Include Employee Representation? Evidence from German
   Corporate Boards, *Journal of Financial Economics* 82, 2006: 673–710.
5 The history of the evolution towards shareholder primacy in the United
   States is described in R. S. Karmel, Should a Duty to the Corporation Be
   Imposed on Institutional Investors? *Business Law* 60, 1, 2004.
6 R. A. G. Monks and N. Minow, *Watching the Watchers*, Cambridge, MA:
   Blackwell Publishers, 1996.
7 For an overview of this research, see M. Huse, *Boards, Governance, and
   Value Creation*, Cambridge University Press, 2007.
8 Cf. based on US data, S. Bhagat and B. Black, The Non-correlation
   Between Board Independence and Long-term Corporate Performance,
   Journal of Corporate Law 27, 2001: 231; based on UK data, C. Weir and
   D. Laing, Governance Structures, Director Independence and Corporate
   Performance in the UK, *European Business Review* 13, 2001: 86–95.
9 See H. Korine, M. Alexander, and P.-Y. Gomez, The Real Job of Boards,
   Business Strategy Review 21 (3), 2010: 36–41, for numerous examples
   of corporate governance failure linked to the inability of independent
   directors to provide an effective check on the designs of managers *and*
   (some) shareholders.
10 As discussed, for example, in the presentation of the Hermes Principles,
   www.ecgi.org/codes/documents/hermes_principles.pdf, and in Peter

Butler's (CEO of Governance for Owners) 2011 address to the 3rd ICSA Corporate Governance Conference, The Future Path of Stewardship, www.governanceforowners.com/images/upload/press_80.pdf.

11 Cf. I. Anabtawi and L. Stout, Fiduciary Duties for Activist Investors, *Stanford Law Review* 60, 2008: 1255.

12 For a thorough discussion of the role of representation in corporate governance, see P.-Y. Gomez and H. Korine, *Entrepreneurs and Democracy: A Political Theory of Corporate Governance*, Cambridge University Press, 2008, chapter 6.

13 Cf. R. C. Anderson and D. M. Reeb, Board Composition: Balancing Family Influence in S&P 500 Firms, *Administrative Science Quarterly* 49, 2004: 209–237.

14 Presentation by Michael Hilti for "Neues VR-Management," Hochschule St. Gallen, Zurich, 2009.

15 As articulated in Gomez and Korine, *Entrepreneurs and Democracy*.

Conclusion – strategy for whom?

1 Our discussion here draws upon that of Mintzberg in his description of the "Power School" in H. Mintzberg, B. Ahlstrand, and J. Lampel, *Strategy Safari*, New York: Free Press, 1998. Like Mintzberg and authors such as MacMillan (I. C. MacMillan, *Strategy Formulation: Political Concepts*, St. Paul: West, 1978), Pettigrew (A. M. Pettigrew, Strategy Formulation as a Political Process, *International Studies of Management and Organization* Summer, 1977: 78–87), and Bower and Doz (J. L. Bower and Y. Doz, Strategy Formulation: A Social and Political Process, in D. E. Schendel and C. W. Hofer [eds.], *Strategic Management*, Boston: Little, Brown, 1979: 152–166), we recognize that strategic decision-making involves a process of political negotiation among executives. Where we differ from these authors is in explicitly considering the impact of shareholders on the process and conceptualizing strategic change as the result of the interaction between and among executives and shareholders.

2 Drawing upon L'Expansion and Agence France Presse in their editions of September 11, 2012.

3 Cf. R. P. Rumelt, *Good Strategy Bad Strategy*, New York: Crown Business, 2011.

Index